TO I .

' should be ret
displayed in the

0/10/02.

To the gay laugh of my mother
At the gate of the grave
(Seán O'Casey)

SEÁN O'CASEY

The Plough
and
the Stars

with introduction, textual notes, commentaries
and workshop activities by
SEÁN MOFFATT

GILL AND MACMILLAN

Published in Ireland by
Gill and Macmillan Ltd
Goldenbridge
Dublin 8
with associated companies throughout the world
© Introduction, textual notes, commentaries and workshop
activities, Seán Moffatt, 1987
7171 1452 X
Print origination in Ireland by The Caseroom, Dublin

CONTENTS

THE EDITOR

Seán Moffatt, B.A., studied and taught at Coláiste Eoin, Finglas, Dublin and has a particular interest in theatre in education. He has directed and acted in numerous stage productions and was artistic director of Trapdoor Theatre Company which toured Ireland with shows for schools and theatres. His own one-act play *There is no Night* was awarded first place in the A.I.B. sponsored play-writing competition and was performed during the Dublin Theatre Festival. He has also written a number of popular radio drama serials for children for RTE, including *The Golden One* and *The Beastly Birdcatchers and the Bushy Bearded Goblins.*

ILLUSTRATIONS

Cover. From an Abbey Theatre production of *The Plough and the Stars*, with Pat Laffan as Lieut. Langon, Pat Layde as Jack Clitheroe and Geoffrey Golden as Captain Brennan (*G.A. Duncan*)

The illustrations which accompany the text of the play are by Fergus Bourke, from the Abbey Theatre's Golden Jubilee production in 1976. For further details see page 38.

Seán O'Casey, dramatist (1880-1964)

INTRODUCTION

O'CASEY'S DUBLIN

Seán O'Casey was born in Dublin on 30 March 1880, at 85 Lower Dorset Street. A lower-class Protestant—like Bessie Burgess in the play—in a predominantly Catholic Dublin, he lived, along with thousands of others, in the grinding poverty of the tenement houses. Seán, whose original name was John Casey, was the last of thirteen children, eight of whom had already died in infancy in a city reputed to have the second-highest death rate in Europe. Michael, Seán's father, worked as a clerk, earning a modest salary. Raising a large family, he barely managed to get by, having to resort to living in the poorer sections of the city.

But things were to get worse for the Casey family. Michael died suddenly, of a spinal injury. Gradually, his wife and five surviving children were further reduced to the penury and hardship of tenement life. For Seán, the squalor of the tenements was to become the crucial experience of his life.

Dublin at this period had one of the most underfed, worst-housed and badly paid populations in Europe. Twenty-one thousand families lived in single-room tenements. Patrick Pearse wrote in the IRB publication *Irish Freedom* (October 1913):

> I calculate that one-third of the people of Dublin are underfed; that half the children attending primary schools are ill-nourished . . . I suppose there are 20,000 families in Dublin to whose domestic economy milk and butter are all but unknown; black tea and dry bread are their staple diet. There are many thousand fireless hearth-places in Dublin on the bitterest days of winter.

Those tragic years were, by and large, a part of the tragedy of Irish life. To fully appreciate a play like *The Plough and the Stars*, and indeed the importance of O'Casey as an Irish playwright, an understanding of the political forces at work in Ireland at that time can be of enormous help to us. Such an examination can also shed some light on the complex personality of the playwright, since he himself was very much an active participant in several of the bodies then shaping and formulating a 'new Ireland'. As we shall see, O'Casey's Dublin plays sprang from the contemporary dynamic forces within Irish society, from an urgent need to engage in the process of history. At times he records actual historical events with documentary precision: he quotes

1

word for word from speeches delivered by those in the forefront of Irish politics.

Let us look, then, at O'Casey's life, the politics of the time, and how they shaped and influenced his work.

A monumental change

It has been said that the thirty years between the death of Parnell in 1891 and the signing of the Anglo-Irish Treaty in 1921 flashed with more brilliance, and at the same time were riddled with more disappointment, than any comparable era in our history. Much the same can be said of O'Casey's years in Dublin. He moved in the same pattern of excited expectation followed by grave disappointment. Because of this he became rather sceptical, as his cutting satire and dramatic irony in *The Plough and the Stars* clearly demonstrate. But the change that took place in the outlook of his generation was monumental.

In the 1890s there was little or no hostility towards Ireland's connection with England. People were content that Ireland should remain part of the United Kingdom, retaining English institutions and the English language. By 1921 there was a definite demand for a break with England, and for a more distinct and separate national existence in politics, economics and culture. How and why did such a change take place? O'Casey drops us into the middle period of this transformation, the months leading up to the Easter Rising of 1916, but we will need to return to the years following Parnell's death.

For more than a decade, Parnell had held together the constitutional and revolutionary wings of the nationalist movement. This alliance led to the creation of a strong and well-disciplined home rule party at Westminster. Parnell's superb leadership created conditions that prepared the way for the final stages in the struggle for independence. After his death, however, a great national movement split apart. The result was a decade of political division and ineffectiveness.

Culture instead of politics

With the fall of Parnell, the romantic hero, people became disillusioned with the party politics of home rule, and turned away in disgust from the vicious political squabbling of the 1890s. Instead, they devoted their energies to an array of cultural and seemingly non-political activities. Poetry came to mean more than politics, ideals more than votes.

William Butler Yeats, building on the work of writers such as Thomas Davis, Samuel Ferguson and Standish O'Grady, led one such movement, the Anglo-Irish literary revival. Poets, dramatists and writers, Yeats believed, would cater for the intellectual needs of Ireland,

The tenement house in Dublin where Seán O'Casey was born

and without an intellectual life, he held, nationality could not be preserved. The most talented literary people of the time answered this call: Lady Augusta Gregory, George Russell, Douglas Hyde, John Millington Synge, George Moore, James Stephens and others. They revived and romanticised the early legends and history of Ireland. Cú Chulainn and his heroic feats became the new image of the Irish hero, replacing the lack-lustre home-rulers such as Grattan and O'Connell.

Cathleen Ni Houlihan

Ireland was often treated in literature as an old woman, the "Shan Van Vok" (*Seanbhean Bhocht*) that Fluther refers to in Act II. This poor old woman would be magically transformed into a queen when men with the courage, strength and dedication of a Cú Chulainn thought her worth dying for. Yeats dramatised this idea in his play *Cathleen Ni Houlihan*:

> They shall be remembered for ever,
> They shall be alive for ever,
> They shall be speaking for ever,
> The people shall hear them for ever.

Though it was a purely academic movement, the literary revival had a profound impact both on the nationalists and the more militant separatists.

O'Casey and the Gaelic League

The Gaelic League, another non-political revivalist movement, founded by Douglas Hyde, Eoin MacNeill and Eugene O'Growney in 1893, set its sights on an Irish-speaking nation. They felt that without its own language and customs, recognition of Ireland as a separate nation would never be forthcoming. O'Casey, who as a child had been busily involved in Bible classes and foreign mission work, joined the Gaelic League in his twenties. He taught himself Irish, and in turn began to teach it to others. It was during this period that he changed his name to Seán.

The Gaelic Athletic Association, another revivalist movement, concentrating on the more popular social activities such as sport and dancing, also attracted the young O'Casey, who was reputed to be a promising hurler. He also played in a pipe band, and devoted a great deal of his energies to debating. O'Casey now shared in the popular belief that language, literature, music, games, dress and ideas all needed to be de-Anglicised.

From culture to politics

But it was impossible for the Gaelic League to remain above politics, propagating, as it did, national self-reliance and self-respect. In fact the league became a well-organised nation-wide pressure group. It demonstrated that Ireland was a cultural nation: and therefore, went the argument, Ireland was entitled to become a nation-state. In other words, it provided the best argument to date for such recognition.

Cultural pursuits gave way to political objectives. O'Casey became a fervent nationalist. In fact it was his involvement with the nationalist cause that created a clash with his religious activities (which we will look at later). The important thing to notice is that while still in his early twenties, O'Casey found himself caught up in two of the most vital aspects of Irish life: religion and politics. And although he worked by day at poorly paid back-breaking jobs such as railway navvy and road digger, he still managed to throw himself with great vigour into debates, games, amateur dramatics (which he wrote for and acted in) and other activities.

Arthur Griffith's Sinn Féin, the Irish Republican Brotherhood (IRB) and James Connolly's socialist movement were among some of the political groups affected by the Gaelic League's philosophy. O'Casey joined the IRB, having fallen out with the Gaelic League for class reasons. This is how Desmond Ryan describes his behaviour at a Sinn Féin meeting:

> Seán O'Casey sits in silence at the back of the hall during the lecture, a dour and fiery figure swathed in labourer's garb, for he works on the railways just then. His neck and throat are bound in the coils of a thick white muffler, and he looks a Jacobin of Jacobins as his small, sharp and red-rimmed eyes stab all the beauty and sorrow of the world. He speaks first, and very fluently in Irish, then launches out into a violent Republican oration in English, stark and forceful, Biblical in diction with gorgeous tints of rhetorics and bursts of anti-English Nationalism of the most uncompromising style. (*Remembering Sion.*)

The IRB attracted many eager young nationalists like O'Casey who had been, in the words of Pearse, schooled in the Gaelic League: people like Pearse himself, MacDonagh, Plunkett and Ceannt—all ill-fated signatories of the 1916 Proclamation.

The IRB suffered from certain internal divisions. Though there were those—the majority—who did not consider rebellion feasible in the circumstances, there were those who looked to the day when England would become involved in a war, and thus provide Ireland with an opportunity. Weeks after the outbreak of the First World War, Tom Clarke and Patrick Pearse were among those who resolved to assert Irish independence before it ended.

Patrick Pearse

Pearse appears in *The Plough and the Stars* as the figure silhouetted in the pub window of Act II. O'Casey sums up Pearse's philosophy by skilfully knitting together a number of key sentences taken from his political writings and speeches. Pearse had been influenced by the cult of bloodshed in Europe over the previous two decades. He saw war as being a good thing in itself. He believed the heart of the world would be refreshed by the 'red wine of the battle fields'. And he likewise believed that the 'heart of Ireland' would be refreshed. 'There has been nothing more terrible in Irish history than the failure of the last generation'. A 'blood sacrifice' would be needed to redeem this failure.

That O'Casey does not support such a philosophy is made evident by the manner in which it is presented to us. Pearse is placed in the background of a pub where, as far as the characters are concerned, more important things are happening. By his ingenious use of dramatic irony, he counterpoints Pearse's talk of heroic warfare with the petty squabbling and harangues of the pub's occupants. In so doing he gives us an accurate impression of the attitude the common people had to such rhetoric.

As we can gather from his treatment of Pearse, O'Casey quickly lost his violent nationalist enthusiasm in the light of such a bloody philosophy. He felt that the leaders, though brave and sincere, were not alive to the problems of the common man, and that they paid little heed to the rough energy and splendour of the working class. It wasn't long before he involved himself in a different kind of revolution, which was running its course independently of the IRB.

O'Casey as Socialist

Marx, Engels and Lenin, ever watchful of Ireland, allowed for the possibility that a socialist revolution overthrowing the existing social order might well be instigated in Ireland. The events of 1913 encouraged this belief.

The fiery Jim Larkin, assisted by James Connolly, organised the Irish Transport and General Workers' Union in an effort to improve the conditions of the working class. William Martin Murphy, in opposition to Larkin, organised 400 employers into a federation, and in August 1913 Larkin's members were locked out. By September, twenty-four thousand workers were out of work. The conflict lasted eight months. There were massive rallies; baton charges by police; a

Jim Larkin addressing a Labour meeting in Dublin

James Connolly

The statue of Cú
Chulainn, the
legendary Irish
hero, which stands
in the General Post
Office, Dublin

number of deaths; riots, arrests, imprisonments; food ships from English sympathisers; and sympathetic strikes.

Larkin was, for O'Casey, nothing short of a truly heroic figure. He saw that Larkin was, unlike the IRB, directly in contact with the needs of the poor and underprivileged. Through Larkin he saw a way in which he could serve both Ireland and Labour. He lost his job for refusing to sign a document undertaking not to join Larkin's union. He became a leader in the union and helped the workers to carry on work without the support of the employers. He helped to organise socials at Liberty Hall for the locked-out workers. Still living with his mother, O'Casey survived on bread and tea purchased with her meagre pension.

There was another clash with the church at this point. Arrangements had been made to send the strikers' children to England where they would be fed and cared for. Fearing that the children might be taught 'pagan' ways, the church intervened and prevented this. This calls to mind one of Fluther's lines, a sentiment O'Casey probably shared with him: 'We ought to have as great a regard for religion as we can, so as to keep it out of as many things as possible'.

Whether or not there were winners in the strike is debatable. What is important is the strong spirit of militancy that had been aroused, which effectively added to the revolutionary climate.

The Irish Citizen Army
The ITGWU had formed its own army, the Irish Citizen Army (of which Clitheroe and Brennan are both members in the play), in order to protect its members from police brutality. O'Casey became secretary of the Citizen Army but, as with religion, the Gaelic League, and nationalism, the inevitable falling out occurred. While Larkin was imprisoned in the United States, O'Casey argued with Connolly over uniforms for the Citizen Army. In Act II The Covey, referring to Peter Flynn, says:

> When I think of all th' problems in front o' th' workers, it makes me sick to be lookin' at oul' codgers goin' about dhressed up like green accoutred figures gone asthray out of a toyshop!

James Connolly
This really sums up O'Casey's argument with Connolly, though Peter's costume far outshines that of the Citizen Army. O'Casey finally resigned from the army when Countess Markievicz was permitted to be a member both of the nationalist Irish Volunteers and the Citizen

Army. O'Casey simply could not reconcile nationalism with the plight of the workers.

Connolly on the other hand was both a nationalist and a socialist. When English workers showed little interest in aiding Irish workers, he put his trust in the establishment of an Irish republic by Irish workers. He wrote: 'The cause of labour is the cause of Ireland, the cause of Ireland is the cause of labour'. O'Casey did not agree. Connolly was resolved on an insurrection and believed that military success was possible. Though the Citizen Army was only 300 strong, in his opinion once the first blow was struck the rest of the country would rise in support. The Covey, who is very much O'Casey's spokesman in the play, sums up the reason why he opposed Connolly on this question. In Act I The Covey tells Clitheroe that the Citizen Army flag is being abused, and goes on to explain:

> Because it's a labour flag an' was never meant for politics . . . what does the design of th' field plough mean, if it's not Communism? It's a flag that should only be used when we're buildin' th' barricades to fight for a Workers' Republic!

The Citizen Army together with the IRB began to formulate a common policy with the aim of freeing Ireland from British rule. O'Casey, as with The Covey, saw this move as a betrayal of the workers on the part of the Citizen Army. He had no choice but to resign.

Political fusion

Thus we begin to get a picture of the historical period and events with which *The Plough and the Stars* deals: a turbulent period in which a number of small dynamic groups—the literary revival, the Gaelic League, the GAA, Sinn Féin, the IRB and the labour movement —not much concerned with electoral or parliamentary success, pursued some social, cultural or political ideal, and converged into a single unit of great power. This was the force that brought about the change in the mental climate and which O'Casey's play so expertly manages to capture on stage with great subtlety.

Pearse at Wolfe Tone's graveside in 1913 and O'Donovan Rossa's in 1915 are two examples of the synthesis of the cultural and political separatists' traditions. Displaying the influence of the Gaelic League, Pearse opened his speeches in Irish. (Note that, as we have already seen, O'Casey behaved in a similar way before he broke away from the IRB.) At Tone's grave, Pearse spoke of the sorrowful destiny of the heroes who turn their backs on the pleasant paths for Ireland's sake, calling to mind the words of Cathleen Ni Houlihan. Connolly would have approved, as would Sinn Féin: the ideals of the literary revival, the Gaelic League, the IRB, Sinn Féin, the Irish Volunteers (Pearse was also a Volunteer) and Connolly's socialist republic in clear fusion.

In 1914 there were five armies in Ireland: the British army (which could hardly be relied upon after the Curragh 'Incident'); and the unofficial armies: the Ulster Volunteers, the Irish Volunteers, the Citizen Army, and the IRB. Something had to give: with the outbreak of war, it did. When the Easter Rising took place O'Casey, having dissociated himself from the Citizen Army, took no part in it. He was imprisoned for a night in St Barnabas' Church—much the same fate as those at the end of the play—and later detained in a granary.

O'CASEY AS WRITER

Estranged from the Labour movement, and just about every other movement, O'Casey slowly began to drift towards a literary career, writing songs and political ballads. He wrote a short history of the Citizen Army and in 1919 *The Frost in the Flower*, the first of several plays he submitted to the Abbey Theatre only to have them rejected.

But 1919 also saw the death of the person who had undoubtedly been the strongest influence in his life—his mother. She had been a devoted mother, of a genteel disposition. The long years of poverty and hunger eventually wore her out. It was a bitter blow for him: she had been the one person he knew he could rely on; she alone had cared for and protected him. This accounts for his portraits in the Abbey plays of women as strong-willed, determined fighters, much more capable of heroic acts than the men.

A number of O'Casey's writings from this period were later developed and incorporated into *The Plough and the Stars. The Crimson and the Tricolour* was another play rejected by the Abbey: one of the characters of this play, though, was later elaborated and became The Covey. *The Cooing of Doves*, a one-act play also rejected by the Abbey, afterwards became the second act of the *Plough. The Shadow of a Gunman*, the first play to be accepted, was performed at the Abbey Theatre on 12 April 1923. After this came his equally successful *Juno and the Paycock* (1925), which preceded the *Plough* by one year.

All three plays, commonly known as the Abbey trilogy, are set precisely in history: each exists under the shadow of an important historic event.

Police baton charge striking workers in Dublin in 1913

Irish Citizen Army soldiers outside Liberty Hall, the Head Office of the ITGWU, at the outbreak of World War I in 1914

The 'Plough' and the Rising

O'Casey's interpretation of the rising was greeted by riots in the theatre, as was Synge's *The Playboy of the Western World* before him. In a sense he had done for the city what Synge had done for the country, extracting elements of poetry, wit, fluency, rhythm and colour of slum speech and using it to form a composite picture of reality. But, also like Synge, he displeased the patriots when he juxtaposed comedy and sacred objects of national veneration. The sight of the national flag in a pub or a prostitute on stage (Dublin then had a thriving red-light district) was more than people could take. But his great achievement was to present major events from recent Irish history from the point of view of the people living in the slum tenements, those he knew so well and cared most about: common, unheroic people unwillingly caught up in civil war and revolution. By presenting history from this new perspective, that of the poor, the low-life braggarts, drunks and wasters forever wrangling about issues they hardly understand, O'Casey found he could expose many of the myths and ideals of Romantic Ireland.

In Act IV of the *Plough* Captain Brennan, speaking of those looting and plundering the city centre shops damaged by the fighting, says to Jack Clitheroe:

> **Capt. Brennan** (*savagely to* Clitheroe). Why did you fire over their heads? Why didn't you fire to kill?
>
> **Clitheroe.** No, no, Bill; bad as they are they're Irish men an' women.
>
> **Capt. Brennan** (*savagely*). Irish be damned! Attackin' an' mobbin' th' men that are risking their lives for them. If them slum lice gather at our heels again, plug one o' them, or I'll soon shock them with a shot or two meself!

O'Casey, as we have seen, left the Citizen Army precisely because he saw that their ideals meant nothing to the starving masses. Here he dramatises, with tragic irony, this very gulf, topples the myth that the Citizen Army were fighting, as they believed, for the people. The 'slum lice' are supposed to be the people Brennan is protecting. Such a scene was not merely invented by O'Casey for dramatic effect. Though the rising was carried out in the name of the Irish people, the fact of the matter was that the people were, at the time, hostile to the fighting.

One account of the events tells us the following:

Pubs and bars were particularly attractive, of course, but soon many other stores had been broken into; and James Connolly was in a quandary. These were the poor and starving of Ireland, the people he had pawned his life for; but he could not stand by and see them bring disgrace on the rising. He ordered his men to fire over the heads of the looters, and when that was ineffective they were forced to fire into the crowd.
(Redmond Fitzgerald, *Cry Blood, Cry Erin*.
Barrie and Rockliff, 1966.)

The British troops, many of them Irish, were cheered as they moved in to attack the rebels. In some areas the National Volunteers came to the assistance of the police and military. It was only after the leaders were executed that feelings changed into veneration for the fallen leaders and respect and support for their surviving comrades. O'Casey's feelings had not changed, and so he found himself at odds with his audience. He was not willing to rewrite history, preferring to confront it, to dig down to the very heart of what it is that drives history: its dynamics.

Dreams and Ideals
Gladstone said men ought not to suffer from disenchantment since ideals in politics are never realised. Though the years following the treaty of 1921 showed a solid achievement and improvement—in trade unions, commercial enterprise, the GAA and the Gaelic League—none of the dreams or ideals were ever really fulfilled. No Gaelic League's Irish-speaking nation, no Yeats's literary-conscious people, nor the republic of the IRB, nor the workers' republic of Connolly. The main characters of *The Plough and the Stars* are dreamers. They dream in order to cope with a bitterly harsh reality. Their tragedy is that they are victims of other people's dreams which for no apparent reason have been forced upon them. At the end of the play one question still demands of us an answer: 'Is there anybody goin', Mrs. Clitheroe, with a titther o' sense?'

After writing *The Plough and the Stars* O'Casey moved to England where he married Eileen Carey, a young Irish actress. His next play, *The Silver Tassie*, was rejected by the Abbey for no good reason. On the same day his first child was born. He settled in Devon, though he based many of his later plays on events and controversies he read of in Irish papers. His subsequent plays were more 'poetic' and experimental, the characters more simplified, the speech less natural. But he seems to have put most of his energy into his six volumes of autobiography. The

Abbey plays are still more or less regarded as being his best work and are well established in the classical repertoire. Not a great amount of excitement has been caused by his later plays.

Influences on O'Casey

When O'Casey's first play was accepted and performed at the Abbey, it was 1923. He was 43 years of age. His life, as we have seen, had consisted of periods of passionate devotion to one or another cause, each of these causes failing to live up to his expectations. He moved from the Church to the Gaelic League, to the IRB and nationalism, to Larkin and the Citizen Army. He became sceptical of and passionate against the orthodoxies of Gaelic nationalism, the Catholic puritanism of the new state, the myth and the rhetoric of violence and the random suffering it inflicted. His personal disillusionment with politics and the concept of Ireland liberated by force gave rise to what is essentially a biting satire. In *The Plough and the Stars* he satirises Pearse and his mystical rhetoric of blood-letting, Peter Flynn's pompous nationalist strutting, Clitheroe's inability to recognise the difference between vanity and heroism, The Covey's hollow advocacy of the international class war above the national struggle. His ability to explode such myths and stupidity came from his own direct and painful experiences on both sides of the fence: as an active campaigner and as one of the common people. It seems that some of his earlier plays had been refused by the Abbey because they attempted to pour scorn on the vices of the rich, about which he knew nothing. It was only after Yeats advised him to write of life as he knew it that the tenements became the settings of his plays, resulting in such wonderful masterpieces. But there were a number of other factors that contributed to the successful formula O'Casey finally hit upon.

The early years

O'Casey had always had a leaning towards literary pursuits although he was plagued by painful eye trouble from early childhood. Nevertheless, throughout the turbulent political years he continued to educate himself by reading as many books as the little money he had would allow. By his own account he came uninstructed to the stage. This is not strictly true, though in some ways it does account for his instinctive as opposed to formal knowledge of play-writing and the theatre.

His father had been a learned, upright and fearless man with a passion for books. O'Casey inherited many of his father's qualities.

The remains of a tramcar destroyed during the 1916 Rising in Dublin. The soldier on horseback is a Lancer. (see Act III, line 83)

Street barricades in Dublin during the 1916 Rising

While working as a young clerk for Hyridim, Leadim and Company he read enormous numbers of books, ranging from Dickens to Balzac, Darwin to Carlyle, and poets such as Byron, Shelley, Keats, and Goldsmith. Elements of most of these authors can be found in his own writing, but of all the authors he read at this period Shakespeare made the strongest and most lasting impression on him. Shakespeare seemed to open up a new source of life for him. He learned a great deal of his lines by heart, and together with his brother formed the 'Townshend Dramatic Society', which performed in some unused stables. He played such parts as Henry VI, Cassius and Brutus. There are a number of things about *The Plough and the Stars* that we can relate directly to Shakespeare's influence on the author.

Shakespeare

Overall, the play does have a great deal of Elizabethan gusto about it: the same frantic energy is there, the same use of comedy as a device effectively undermining more serious issues, the same breath of sympathy, range of tone, and truth to life.

But we can find more concrete examples of Shakespeare's influence. Nora's insanity, for instance, is almost an exact replica of Ophelia's in *Hamlet*:

> **Ophelia.** There's rosemary, that's for remembrance; pray, love, remember: and there is pansies that's for thoughts . . . There's fennel for you . . . and here's some for me—we may call it herb-grace o' Sundays—O, you must wear your rue with a difference.—There's a daisy—I would give you some violets, but they withered all when my father died—they say, he made a good end—(*sings*) For bonny sweet Robin is all my joy.

No longer able to cope with the pain of separation and the loss of her child, Nora turns, like Ophelia, to lyrical rural memories of courtship:

> **Nora.** No . . . Not there, Jack. . . . I can feel comfortable only in our own familiar place beneath th' bramble tree . . . We must be walking for a very long time; I feel very, very tired . . . Have we to go farther, or have we passed it by? (*Passing her hand over her eyes*) Curious mist on my eyes . . . Why don't you hold my hand, Jack . . . (*Excitedly*) No, no, Jack, it's not. Can't you see it's a goldfinch. Look at th' black-satiny wings with th' gold bars, an' th' splash of crimson on its head.

The character of Fluther in certain respects derives from Shakespeare's Falstaff. Fluther shares with Falstaff an endless line in heroic talk, inferior wit, bold speech, and presumption with cowardice. Compare, for example, Fluther's words to Rosie in Act II—after The Covey, who would probably have downed him without too much trouble, has been evicted by the landlord—with those of Falstaff in *King Henry IV Part One*:

> **Fluther.** I wasn't goin' to let meself be malignified by a chancer . . . He got a little bit too derogatory for Fluther . . . Be God, to think of a cur like that comin' to talk to a man like me!
>
> **Rosie** (*fixing on his hat*). Did j'ever!
>
> **Fluther.** He's lucky he got off safe. I hit a man last week, Rosie, an' he's fallin' yet!

In the following scene Falstaff, who has spent most of the battle avoiding danger, stands over a corpse which he maintains he killed himself:

> **Prince Henry.** Why, Percy I killed myself and saw thee dead.
>
> **Falstaff.** Didst thou?—Lord, Lord, how this world is given to lying!—I grant you I was down and out of breath, and so was he; but we rose both at an instant, and fought a long hour by Shrewsbury clock. If I may be believed, so; if not, let them that should reward valour bear the sin upon their own heads. I'll take it upon my own death, I gave him this wound in the thigh: if the man were alive, and would deny it, zounds, I would make him eat a piece of my own sword.

Falstaff's fictional account of his fight with Percy is not unlike Fluther's somewhat dubious description of a sabre slice that he received from a dragoon in O'Connell Street, or the hole in his head got from a policeman's baton. Though Falstaff is a coward and a villain, we are willing to make allowances, primarily because of his wit and verbal dexterity. Fluther could not be described as an outright coward and a villain in the same mould as Falstaff; nonetheless we do accept his boasting and posing for much the same reasons.

Language

This brings us to O'Casey's use of language, which is often described, mistakenly, as Elizabethan. This is not the place for a detailed analysis of the play's language. Suffice it to say that when O'Casey tries to use poetry as Shakespeare did in his plays, the language becomes noticeably awkward and unreal. Compare the language of the two pieces already quoted above, that of Nora and Ophelia. The language used in the love scene at the end of Act I has the same awkward quality: 'Little, little red-lipped Nora'. Whilst Shakespeare could make poetry sound natural, O'Casey's real forte works in the opposite direction, in that he makes natural speech sound strangely poetic. O'Casey's dialogue is at its strongest when it is selected from the real language of the Dublin slums:

> **Peter** (*leaping to his feet in a whirl of rage*). Now, I'm tellin' you, me young Covey, once and for all, that I'll not stick any longer these tittherin' taunts of yours, rovin' round to sing your slights an' slanders, reddenin' th' mind of a man to th' thinkin' an' sayin' of things that sicken his soul with sin!

or Fluther's beautiful way of telling Nora he has given up drinking:

> **Fluther** (*seriously*). Ne'er a one at all, Mrs Clitheroe, for Fluther's on th' wather waggon now. You could stan' where you're stannin' chantin', 'Have a glass o' malt, Fluther; Fluther, have a glass o' malt,' till th' bells would be ringin' th' ould year out an' th' New Year in, an' you'd have as much chance o' movin' Fluther as a tune on a tin whistle would move a deaf man an' he dead.

These lines are based on the actual words, slang, phrases, rhythms and accents of the streets. O'Casey extracted poetry that was already there, such as alliteration and colourful imagery: it is not how people speak but rather a conscious manipulation of their accents and unique verbal mannerisms.

Dion Boucicault

While the young O'Casey was performing in the 'Townshend Dramatic Society', Boucicault was another favourite playwright. Dion Boucicault (1820-1890) was an Irish dramatist who turned his hand to fashionable melodrama and French comedy. His celebrated plays are *The Colleen Bawn*, *Arrah na Pogue*, and *The Shaughraun*, in which we know O'Casey played a character called Father Dolan.

Boucicault held no political ideas: he was interested first and foremost in successful, entertaining theatre. He used excitement, pathos, comedy and sensational effects for their own sake. As did Synge and George Bernard Shaw, O'Casey greatly admired Boucicault, and in particular his portrait of the Irish rogue. Until Boucicault, the stage Irishman was presented as no more than a stupid heavy drinker;

Boucicault inverted this image. His rogues became charming and patriotic stage Irishmen who were hard drinkers and good talkers, but also cunning enough to outmanoeuvre their aristocratic betters. Characters such as Seán the Post, the Shaughraun, and Myles-Na-Coppaleen, Dublin audiences took to their hearts. O'Casey developed this character, some of whose features can be seen in Fluther, who is fond of his drink, apparently irresponsible though capable of good deeds, and indulges in fine verbal fluency.

But O'Casey's interest in politics and his experiments with form set him in a category apart from Boucicault. Though Boucicault gave his plays a historical setting, these merely served as backdrops against which his sentimental versions of Irish people could act.

We have already touched on O'Casey's encounter with religion while still in his late teens. This encounter was no mere skirmish. Though his faith weakened, religion was to have a lasting influence on his life and work. Very much a rationalist at heart, he came to feel that religion simply could not cater for the grim realities about him. A reading of Darwin's *The Descent of Man* served the final blow, calling to mind The Covey's answer to Fluther when asked about Adam and Eve:

> **The Covey.** Adam an' Eve! Is that as far as you've got? Are you still thinkin' there was nobody in th' world before Adam and Eve? (*Loudly*) Did you ever hear, man, of th' skeleton of th' man o' Java?

However, he had always been drawn to the Bible, as much for its language as for its content. The vocabulary and the rhythms of the King James Bible are all-pervasive in his work. One does not have to look farther than Bessie Burgess to find this influence:

> **Bessie.** Theres' th' men out into th' dhread dimness o' danger, while th' lice is crawlin' about feedin' on th' fatness o' th' land! But yous 'll not escape from th' arrow that flieth be night, or th' sickness that wasteth be day . . . An' ladyship an' all, as some o' them may be, they'll be scattered abroad, like th' dust in th' darkness.

European drama

Another strong influence on O'Casey's work was that of continental European drama. This was to affect the way in which he structured his plays and used theatrical devices. Boucicault, as we have seen, did nothing more than adapt Irish topics to the popular theatrical formula that then prevailed. O'Casey chose to write less conventionally structured plays. He had read the plays of Strindberg and Ibsen, but was particularly impressed by German Expressionism. In this kind of theatre, people are not presented in the traditional way as real-life personalities with easily recognisable psychological traits. Characters come to represent ideas, usually social: of right and wrong, good and evil. It was really in his later plays that O'Casey came to exploit this form. But there is one very striking use of it in *The Plough and the Stars*: the 'figure of a tall man who is speaking to the crowd'.

To all intents and purposes this man is Patrick Pearse, but this we know only because he delivers lines actually written by Pearse. Within the play's structure he is no more than a voice extolling the virtues of war and bloodshed: 'Bloodshed is a cleansing and sanctifying thing'. We cannot describe this figure as a 'character' in the play in the same way as we can Mrs. Gogan or Peter Flynn. The figure in the window of Act II is a device with which the abuse of rhetoric and the assumption that war is a necessary social force are undermined. The use of such a device, and the overall structure of the play, a play without the usual straightforward plot and the normal beginning-middle-end pattern, without any main characters or neatly packaged happy ending—all of these considerations place O'Casey as a thoroughly modern twentieth-century writer.

Categorising O'Casey

Thus, to label O'Casey as a purely 'realist' playwright would be to only partially account for his style. Of the many different forms of theatre— symbolism, expressionism, political, tragi-comedy, absurdism—it is difficult to place O'Casey into any single one. This is very much a result, as this introduction has tried to indicate, of the complex route that brought him to the theatre. The fact of the matter is that O'Casey is partly political, partly comic and tragic, partly farce. He is not averse to characters clowning Chaplin-like on stage: Peter Flynn struggling with his 'thwarting' shirt collar, or left with an abandoned baby while its mother, Mrs. Gogan, goes to battle it out with Bessie Burgess.

In a world of chaos there is always room for music-hall knockabout. Though the author describes the play as a tragedy, a comic spirit often dominates the action. Flashes of wit and rage abound, elaboate insults flow with true spontaneity, the result being an exhilarating fusion of sombre tragedy and boisterous comedy. In the end, the task of trying to apply a suitable label to O'Casey as a playwright is a pointless one.

The failure of institutions

Until he found his true vocation in writing, O'Casey's life had been a series of enthusiasms and disillusionments. Ultimately, he lost faith in all institutions, however worthy their sentiments or intentions. But he never lost faith in people. The tenements of *The Plough and the Stars* were really a loosely organised commune, filled with the hustle and bustle of everyday life, animosities and good will.

There is no closely knit family unit, for instance. Notice how in the opening moments of the play the Clitheroe flat is occupied by Fluther, Peter Flynn and Mrs. Gogan: everybody but the Clitheroes themselves; a sure indication of the communal nature of the tenements. And it is this 'loose' quality of people's relations to each other that contributes to their survival. Nora, in trying to build a family, is really going against this notion. (Symbolically, she is having a lock placed on her door as if to cut herself off from the realities of tenement life.) Her efforts are doomed to failure from the outset as are the other forces that attempt to hold people together in a single institutional unit. The various ideological factions cannot hold together, and serve only to intrude and wreak havoc on those they are supposedly protecting. Whatever good there is in the play comes from the actions of individuals, and evil from the institutions without. Let us then examine more closely some of the principal characters of the play in the light of these considerations.

CHARACTER STUDY

'Your strong point is characterisation,' Lady Gregory told O'Casey after the Abbey had refused *The Crimson and the Tricolour.* He very obviously took heed of her advice and went on to create some of the most memorable characters in modern drama. The interesting thing about *The Plough and the Stars* is that no main character or pair of characters dominates the action as one would normally expect, and indeed as there had been in his previous two plays. The various characters are linked to each other not by choice but by force of circumstance, and thus they find themselves on the same side, involuntarily, in a struggle against the forces of death and destruction. They have no common policy, no abstract ideals, simply an unspoken rule to support each other in times of trouble. Even towards the end of the play we see Brennan, until now very much an outsider, being shielded from the English soldiers by the others.

The characters in general

Each character in the play serves to highlight aspects of other characters as much as of themselves. In talking of one person we cannot ignore his or her relation to one or other of the characters. Thus Mrs. Gogan in the first six minutes of the play manages to give us important information concerning five principal characters, and incidental information concerning some others. We learn of Nora's 'notions of upperosity', Jack's vanity, and the growing tension between the two of them: 'I'm thinkin' he's beginnin' to take things more quietly; the mystery of havin' a woman's a mystery no longer'. She talks of the tension between The Covey and Peter Flynn: 'He an' Th' Covey can't abide each other. There'll be blood dhrawn one o' these days'. More importantly, she tells us how much Nora fears that Jack will return to the Citizen Army: 'She's like a clockin' hen if he leaves her sight for a minute'. Through all this talk, Mrs Gogan displays her own insatiable curiosity, her gossipy nature and her disdain for Nora's attempts at betterment: 'Th' way she thries to be polite', an attitude Fluther does not share with her: 'She's a pretty little Judy all the same'. And this line of Fluther's hints at his amorous nature, an aspect of his personality that we see more fully during Act II in his dealings with Rosie.

Thus an aspect of Mrs. Gogan's character—her love of gossip—is effectively used as a means of informing us of and emphasising the interrelatedness of the lives of these people. People are introduced to us in terms of their connections with others. This seemingly arbitrary opening dialogue between Fluther and Mrs. Gogan is tightly controlled. Taking the characters as a whole, it is designed to shed light on different areas of the play's collective protagonist.

Nora

Looking at Act I, we can safely say that Nora dominates the action, her presence being felt even before Mrs. Gogan mentions her name, by the way in which the room is furnished: 'in a way that suggests an attempt towards a finer expression of domestic life'. It is Nora's hat Mrs. Gogan is impressed by, Nora's husband whose actions bring the act to its climax; it is Nora whom we see controlling Uncle Peter and The Covey in what can only be regarded as a striking reversal of the traditional image of the woman's role. 'God Almighty,' says Mrs. Gogan, 'you'd think th' poor men were undergoin' penal servitude'.

Driven by wilful determination, Nora is more than capable of getting her own way, shrewdly resorting to 'feminine charm' when Jack proves difficult:

> **Nora** (*coaxingly*). I didn't mean to say anything out o' th' way.
> You take a body up too quickly, Jack. (*In an ordinary tone as if*

22

nothing of an angry nature has been said) You didn't offer me
me evenin' allowance yet. (Clitheroe *silently takes out a
cigarette for her and himself and lights both*).

Nora stands out in such strong relief that for a time it looks as if she
may well be the main character. Brennan's entrance, however, brings
with it the first indication that Nora may not be as strong as we have
been led to believe. Once Jack learns of the letter she has hidden, Nora
realises that no amount of 'feminine charm', however cunningly em-
ployed, will effect a change of heart. She flares up:

> 'I burned it! I burned it! That's what I did with it! Is General
> Connolly an' th' Citizen Army goin' to be your only care?'

Nora is not willing to settle for less than Jack's full devotion. By Act
III (her absence in Act II reducing her potential status as a main
character) her determination has turned to desperation. Her character
has weakened significantly and she no longer holds the stage as she did
in Act I. Her off-stage cries of anguish as her baby is being born dead
emphasise literally and figuratively that all life has been killed in
Nora. By Act IV 'her eyes are glimmering with the light of incipient
insanity.'

Nora's strength has also been her weakness. Like those trying to
build a New Ireland out of dreams, Nora's vision of an idyllic family
founders on the rocks of reality. No matter how many doors she fixes
with locks, the outside world insists on intruding. She turns from this
painful realisation and into the insanity she herself anticipated in Act
III when she says to Mrs. Gogan, 'Sometimes, Mrs. Gogan, sometimes I
think I'm goin' mad.'

Nora cannot accept change, she cannot adapt as the others can. And
it is important to note here that none of the characters can be said to
change or develop as the play progresses. With each act, they reveal
aspects of their characters hitherto concealed from us. Bessie Burgess,
for example, who could be said to undergo a complete transformation,
doesn't actually change but brings about a change in our opinion of
her. The Bessie Burgess of Act I who screams at Clitheroe:

> Mind who you're pushin', now . . . I attend me place o' worship
> anyhow . . . not like some o' them that go to neither church,
> chapel nor meetin'-house . . . If me son was home from th'
> threnches he'd see me righted.

remains the same loud-mouthed, stubborn loyalist who moments before her death turns on Corporal Stoddart, who has mistakenly called her a 'Shinner', and tells him:

> Bessie Burgess is no Shinner, an' never had no thruck with anything spotted be th' fingers o' th' Fenians; but always made it her business to harness herself for church whenever she knew that *God Save the King* was goin' to be sung at th' end of the service.

Bessie
As Nora's positive energies decline, Bessie's become more and more apparent. O'Casey expertly manipulates our attitude to Bessie by first presenting her to us in an unfavourable light. Placing Bessie in opposition to Nora in Act I, the author leaves us very little room to feel sympathy for her. This, and the fact that Bessie is a Protestant in a predominantly Catholic environment, causes her to seem isolated from the others.

In Act II Bessie sides with The Covey—who is also in a sense isolated at this moment politically—and launches out at the others in an attack almost purposely designed to assert her differences:

> **Bessie** (*speaking to* The Covey, *but really at the other party*). I can't for th' life o' me undherstand how they can call themselves Catholics, when they won't lift a finger to help poor little Catholic Belgium.

The ensuing verbal battle running up to the physical confrontation between the two women is a direct result of Bessie's deliberate antagonism. Even so it would be wrong to say that the events of this act isolate Bessie all the more. Mrs. Gogan joins in the argument uninvited, and is determined to become involved although Bessie has told her to mind her own business. The two women go to it with such enthusiasm that the result, paradoxically, is a picture of Bessie as a more integrated member of the community than we first suspected. That the two women completed their evening enjoying each other's company in some other public house is not beyond the realms of possibility; especially now that Mrs. Gogan has found a baby-sitter in Peter Flynn.

In this play, squabbling between two people is more a measure of kinship than enmity. The same two women in Act III, following another verbal battle, become as thick as thieves—literally, sharing a pram to loot and plunder the city centre. On returning, they discuss their fashionable new clothes like bosom friends:

> **Mrs. Gogan** (*outside*). I don't remember ever having seen such lovely pairs as them, (*they appear*) with th' pointed toes an' th' cuban heels.

> **Bessie.** They'll go grand with th' dhresses *we're* after liftin', when *we've* stitched a sthray bit o' silk to lift th' bodices up a little bit higher, so as to shake th' shame out o' them, an make them fit for women that hasn't lost themselves in th' nakedness o' th' times. [*Emphasis added.*]

Act III features some contradictory aspects of Bessie's character. Fluther, who was distinctly sympathetic to Bessie in Act I, is driven to roar up at her window, 'Y' ignorant oul' throllope, you.' Brennan responds to her taunts with: 'Shut up y'oul hag!' From her window, Bessie seems to be enjoying the spectacle of suffering and bloodshed inflicted on those who she predicted would 'not escape from th' arrow that flieth be night, or th' sickness that wasteth be day.' Her voice almost echoes that of the figure in the window of Act II, delighting as she does at the sight of her sworn enemies getting their just deserts. 'Judgements are prepared for scorners an' sthripes for th' back o' fools.'

But during the same act, Bessie is seen to slip a mug of milk to Mollser (when she is sure no-one is watching); and it is Bessie who risks her life for Nora by going in search of a doctor amid rifle shots and machine-gun fire. How can we reconcile these seemingly contradictory aspects of Bessie's character?

In short, the answer is that we cannot. Bessie, especially as Act IV demonstrates, is the one truly heroic figure in the play, but she is not a saint. Her character, like that of the others, does not exist in a vacuum; circumstances play a large part in determining her behaviour. Thus one moment she boasts of her high morals and exemplary religious practices, the following she dashes into the streets to pilfer from the unfortunate shopkeepers; she shouts hurtful abuse at Nora, threatens to 'paste' her face, yet runs to her aid; she vociferates her superior ancestry (English Protestant), but attacks Nora because she is 'always thrying to speak proud things, an' lookin' like a mighty one in th' congregation o' th' people!'

Bessie's character is by far the most complex one in the play, and this in turn makes her all the more credible. Her strength is not a product of the supernatural, it is human. And being human, Bessie also has her faults. O'Casey is not trying to topple the conventional ideas of heroism by replacing them with some godly portrait. Bessie does what she has to do, given the circumstances. It is no surprise that people run to her room for protection. Both Fluther and Mrs. Gogan are the first to acknowledge that they have known all along of Bessie's good points, though both have also been more than willing to condemn her weaknesses. After Bessie has shielded Nora with her own body from the gunfire, we are witness to this inherent contradiction. She cries out: 'I've got this through . . . through you . . . through you, you bitch, you . . . O God, have mercy on me!' Forgiveness, hatred, fear—Bessie is not in short supply of any of these. She is essentially human, no more, no less.

At the play's outset we mistake Bessie for a virtueless harridan; at the close of the play she is mistaken for a sniper. Her death, paralleled by Nora's spiritual death, is truly heroic—unlike the pretentious 'gleam of glory' that marked Jack's death.

Fluther

Like Bessie and Nora, Fluther Good is an essential part of the tenement unit rather than the central figure of the play. But, like Bessie, Fluther grows in stature as the play progresses: from the seemingly irresponsible comedian to a serious, caring individual.

In Act I, Fluther is an unfortunate victim of Mrs. Gogan's colourful musings on the subject of death:

> **Fluther** (*faintly*). A man in th' pink o' health should have a holy horror of allowin' thoughts o' death to be festherin' in his mind, for—(*with a frightened cough*) be God, I think I'm afther gettin' a little catch in me chest that time—it's a creepy thing to be thinkin' about.

This is Fluther the clown, the fall guy, and a feature of Fluther's character O'Casey obviously takes great delight in portraying. Notice his opening description of Fluther's physical appearance:

> '. . . nose bent . . . bald, save for a few peeping tufts of reddish hair around his ears . . . a scrubby red moustache . . . dressed in a seedy black suit . . . wears a respectable little black bow . . . On his head a faded jerry hat, which, when excited, he has a habit of knocking farther back on his head, in a series of taps.'

Significantly, there is an unmistakable similarity to Laurel and Hardy, or more accurately Charlie Chaplin, in Fluther's looks and dress. Fluther lives up to this image in his behaviour as well as in his words. (We have already touched on some of Fluther's antecedents in Shakespeare and Boucicault.) He delivers some of the best one-liners: 'I feel as dizzy as bedamned! I hope I didn't give up th' beer too suddenly', and 'I think we ought to have as much respect for religion as we can, so as to keep it out of as many things as possible', and 'I hit a man last week, Rosie, an' he's fallin' yet.' And when, in Act IV, Sergeant Tinley complains that by using a sniper the Irish are not fighting fair, Fluther retorts: 'Fight fair! A few hundred scrawls o' chaps with a couple o' guns an' Rosary beads, again a hundred thousand trained men with horse, fut, an' artillery . . . an' he wants us to fight fair? D'ye want us to come out in our skins an' throw stones?'

Fluther the clown reaches a high point when in Act II he plays the quixotic defender of Rosie's reputation against The Covey's vindictive tongue. Fortunately for Fluther, the barman intervenes before the first blow is struck. Nonetheless Fluther, encouraged by Rosie, talks of the event as if he has scored a victory, as if The Covey had left the bar with his tail between his legs. 'I wasn't goin' to let meself be malignified by a chancer . . . He got a little bit too derogatory for Fluther . . . Be God, to think of a cur like that comin' to talk to a man like me!' This last phrase of Fluther's—'a man like me'—is a key to understanding his character, in that it expresses Fluther's positive image of himself. Earlier in the same act he says: 'Get th' Dublin men goin' an' they'll go on full force for anything that's thryin' to bar them away from what they're wantin'.' Fluther, naturally, regards himself as an exemplary specimen of 'Dublin men'.

But what we know of Fluther would not seem to agree with this image. We know he has a drink problem: the author tells us, Fluther tells us, and we see him drunk twice. He boasts and brags about his injuries received in the name of Ireland, but shows no signs of wishing to become involved in the actual fighting. There is, then, an enormous difference between our image of Fluther and the image he has of himself, the net result being one of comic relief. One cannot help but find Fluther's challenge to the two English soldiers in Act IV amusing: 'Jasus, you an' your guns. Leave them down an' I'd beat the two o' yous without sweatin',' or his line to The Covey: 'Let him go, let him go, Tom: let him open the door to sudden death if he wants to!'

He is a poseur but, for all that, a sincere poseur, in marked contrast to Peter Flynn. And when the mock heroism gives way momentarily to complete abandon, with Fluther crying out at the end of Act III: 'Th' whole city can topple home to hell, for Fluther', it does not affect our opinion of him in a negative way. His whole world is toppling down, and not even the rebels can do anything about it.

But that is Fluther the clown. There is also the Fluther who spends the night, at considerable risk to himself, searching for Nora among the blood-strewn barricades, thus displaying real courage and affection. In Act IV Mrs. Gogan says of Fluther:

> I'll never forget what you done for me, Fluther, goin' around at th' risk of your life settlin' everything with th' undhertaker an' th' cemetery people. When all me own were afraid to put their noses out, you plunged like a good one through hummin' bullets, an' they knockin' fire out o' th' road, tinklin' through th' frightened windows, an' splashin' themselves to pieces on th' walls! An' you'll find that Mollser, in th' happy place she's gone to, won't forget to whisper, now an' again, th' name o' Fluther.

How do we reconcile these very considerable qualities of the man with those of Fluther the clown, the braggart, the drunk? Again, as we found in Bessie's case, we simply cannot. Nora describes Fluther as a 'whole man', and it is the whole man we come to know: his strengths and weaknesses. Also like Bessie, Fluther is a rather complex character. It is difficult to know, for instance, just how much truth there is in his boasting. Had The Covey not been evicted from the bar at the crucial moment, might Fluther have taken his chances and battled it out? Had the two soldiers accepted his challenge, might Fluther have gone to it with both fists at the ready? He does not take part in the armed struggle about which he demonstrates such enthusiasm, but then if he were to do so we would probably regard him in the same negative light as Brennan and Jack Clitheroe. Of his drinking, we are told by the author that he is 'determined to conquer the habit before he dies.' This statement in itself is ambiguous since we also know Fluther's will-power to be weak.

The only certain thing we can safely say of Fluther—because the author tells us, and Fluther amply demonstrates it in the course of the play—is that he is a man 'rarely surrendering to thoughts of anxiety.' In other words, amid destruction and relentless disintegration his is a positive force. Like the harmless tramp of the silent movies, whom he so much resembles, Fluther is a little man with a big heart, his whole life at odds with the toppling world about him. Ultimately his character serves to undermine the shallow ideals of people like Captain Brennan and their delusions of grandeur. Brennan deserts Jack in his hour of need; Fluther the drunk, the clown, the boaster and poseur, unceremoniously runs to Nora's aid. When we speak of the play presenting a new version of heroism, we must look to Fluther as well as to Bessie.

As has already been pointed out, the events in the play do not so much bring about a change in the characters as they do in our perceptions of them. We are enlightened more than they are. Mrs. Gogan may seem to be displaying a change of heart when she acknowledges Bessie's kind treatment of Mollser, but this she has known about all along. By Act IV The Covey does seem to have attained a slightly more humane outlook than his previous cliché-ridden phrases indicated. He says of Mollser: 'Sure she never got any care. How could she get it, an' th' mother out day an' night lookin' for work, an' her consumptive husband leavin' her with a baby to be born before he died.' But this does not really argue in favour of a change in his outlook. It is surely The Covey's knowledge of such deprivation that has driven him to socialism, as it did O'Casey. Little has changed about The Covey, one of whose last lines in the play, delivered to Corporal Stoddart, is: 'Fight for your country! Did y' ever read, comrade, Jenersky's *Thesis on the Origin, Development, an' Consolidation of th' Evolutionary Idea of the Proletariat?*'

Peter Flynn remains the same belligerent crank throughout the play. Each appearance confirms our worst suspicions of him as a character. He has all the hallmarks of a spoilt child, constantly at war with the others and blaming all the world's wrongs on them rather than himself. He does not just want to impress other people, as Fluther does at times, but regards others as inferior to him. While, for example, Fluther admits he should try to give up drink, Peter regards himself above any such reproach. He does not have the sincerity, humour, or good will of Fluther. More than being a portrayal of a complex human character, Peter is used as a means of satire. His uniform with its plumes and unwieldy sword, emblems of legendary days, are no more than toys in the hands of a child.

Nor is The Covey a fully developed character. Apart from taunting Peter, he spends most of his time on stage mouthing hollow socialist jargon. We know that O'Casey fervently believed in the sentiments expressed by The Covey. It is through The Covey, as we have seen, that O'Casey makes his views on the Citizen Army's participation in the rising known. And through The Covey, O'Casey manages to make a strong case against those who would use words without feelings to try to cure the world. But The Covey as a person we never really come to know. He delivers a few key lines, adding yet another important dimension to the play and its many themes, but he then fades into the background. We do not come to know him in the same intimate detail as Nora, Bessie or Fluther.

Mrs. Gogan

Mrs. Gogan's love of idle gossip is made full use of, as we have already observed, in the openings of Acts I and III. But her fascination with death is another of her outstanding traits. Death is seen to be a mysterious and romantic thing. Each of the characters has his or her own way of coping with reality: this is Mrs. Gogan's. The frequency of deaths in her own family and of those about her have brought with them a need to somehow comprehend it in an acceptable form. Death personified in this manner helps to ease the pain and gloss over the sadness. Thus in Act IV we are told she is 'a little proud of the importance of being directly connected with death.'

She is more typical of the tenement women than Bessie, primarily because she is a Catholic. But though she has more lines than any other character in the play, she never really holds our attention to the same degree as Bessie or even Nora. We cannot say that she has any particularly noteworthy features outside her insatiable curiosity, her gossip, and this morbid fascination for death.

Jack Clitheroe

Finally Jack Clitheroe. What we know of Nora's husband has as much to do with what we are told as it has with what we see of him. Clearly O'Casey uses him to further his attack on the notion of the Citizen Army as an appropriate body of people to fight a war. Two things are made clear about Jack: he is attracted to the glory as opposed to the ideals of the Citizen Army; and his interest in Nora is beginning to wane. Both of these factors, the former aggravating the latter, precipitate his death, the nature of which we can only ascertain from Brennan's dubious account. Jack is a minor figure among a host of other minor figures such as Brennan, Langon, Stoddart and Tinley. Any interest in Jack Clitheroe rests on the effects his actions have on Nora more than on the personality of Jack himself.

THEMES OF "THE PLOUGH AND THE STARS"

On Themes

It is always difficult to single out any one 'message' or 'theme' in a full-length play. A play, after all, is not like a poem that tends to build itself around one theme such as love, death, time, or loneliness. A play is more likely to take all of these themes and more, building up into a complex network of ideas and contradictions.

The *Plough* is no exception in this respect. From start to finish it moves from one argument to the next and back again without ever seeming to come to any conclusions. Often, we have to look beyond what the characters actually say to get at the playwright's true meaning. Socialism, nationalism, religion, heroism—these are the most obvious themes of the *Plough*; and in his essentially ironic treatment of each of these, O'Casey presents us with a number of alternative interpretations. But the most important theme of the play is one we might easily overlook, since it is implied rather than directly stated: this theme is human nature, with all its inconsistencies and ambiguities.

People as a Theme

More than anything else, O'Casey's characters dominate the play. It is their indomitable personalities, their courage and strength of character that holds our attention and forces all the other issues into the background. For O'Casey, the people are the theatre. He tells us in an essay that

> Nature sets the scene, and man plays his part through the changing scenes of seed-time and harvest, in the cold days when the frost comes and the keen winds blow. It is from the things manifested in people's life—their love, joy, hatred, malice, envy, generosity, passion, courage, and fear—that the truest playwrights weave their sombre and gay patterns of action and dialogue. Every art is rooted in the life of the people—what they see, do, how they hear, all they touch and taste; how they live, love and go to the grave.

Society is made up of many individuals. Politics, religion, economics—these are merely reflections of what 'people' are. If we are to understand such social phenomena, then some understanding of human nature must come first. The *Plough* concentrates on *character*, on the *individual*, because it is only through him or her than an insight into the period and the real issues that were at stake can be gained.

Although O'Casey implies that we can never fully appreciate or come to terms with human nature, there is nonetheless the very definite belief that the individual is always superior to any set of ideals, be they social, political, religious, or otherwise.

No matter how grandiose the subject at hand may seem, there are

31

always certain basic human needs to be accounted for. Against the colourful, exciting picture of war, as given by the silhouetted figure in Act II, there is Nora's moving description of a young, dead rebel's twisted body. Against the call for a new heroism, there is the deplorable poverty of which Mollser's death is a result. Against the call for patriotism, there is Fluther's 'Th' whole city can topple home to hell.' The people themselves and their reactions: this is O'Casey's theme; all the other issues follow on from this.

Tragedy and Comedy

Before taking a closer look at some of the more general themes of the *Plough*, it is necessary to make O'Casey's *tragi-comic* vision of humanity clear. It is this duality that ultimately gives the play its irony.

As the quotation above indicates, O'Casey believed the playwright should depict *both* the pain and the joy experienced by the individual, the way in which he or she copes in a society that never seems to get it right. For this reason, the *Plough* is neither exact tragedy nor pure comedy; instead, it is a combination of both. Scenes of low comedy may precede, follow, or even merge with scenes of profound tragedy. Amid the preposterous scenes of looting in Act III, for example, Langon is carried in dying in agony from a stomach wound. In Act IV the men argue, bicker and play cards beside a coffin containing Nora's stillborn baby and Mollser.

O'Casey refuses to ignore the suffering and wretchedness of the people he portrays, but he also refuses to indulge in despair. We are given a picture of the war between hope and despair with the inflicted laughing in the face of adversity. O'Casey once said: 'Shakespeare does not stay very long with his sorrows; he sings and dances even in the midst of them.' Shakespeare was a playwright from whom O'Casey learned a great deal.

Irony

It is precisely this contradictory vision that brings about the *irony* of the play. At the heart of irony, especially as used by O'Casey, there is always some form of contradiction. Either what a person says contradicts what he or she does, or two actions are seen to be in conflict. Irony allows O'Casey to place the conflicting emotions of pain and humour side by side. It is used to attack and to celebrate. As we shall see, this irony informs the playwright's treatment of the play's general themes.

Socialism

Given that The Covey is the one advocate of socialism in the *Plough*, O'Casey's intentional irony is not difficult to recognise. What The Covey has to say may seem to make sense, and indeed a great deal of what he says may be attributed to O'Casey's own socialist beliefs. There is, however, the problem of context. What, for example, is the point of telling Rosie in Act II that 'conthrol o' th' means o' production, rates of exchange an' th' means of disthribution is man's only hope of salvation'? He is talking to the wrong person, at the wrong time, and in the wrong place. And so we get this conflict between the seriousness of what The Covey has to say and the ludicrous moments he chooses to say it. But socialism itself is not the target of O'Casey's irony, rather it is the blindness of those who cannot recognise the gulf that exists between theory and practice. In theory, 'equality for all' is most commendable, but of no immediate use to a starving family. The Covey is under the impression that socialism is the answer to all evils, and cannot understand why nobody is bothered to listen to him. He is not aware of the fact that they already *know* what he is telling them. They know there are those who are better off; they know they are exploited by employers and politicians; they know the society they live in is corrupt and unjust, and that things could be a lot better. If The Covey were to put his book and his theories away, and started telling people what could be *done* to change things, then his words might not fall on deaf ears. (This is one reason why the orator of Act II is received with such enthusiasm. Here is someone promising to *do* something.)

O'Casey regarded socialism as a humane system of politics arising out of people's needs. His depiction of tenement people gathered together in an effort to protect one another from the overwhelming chaos about them is in itself a picture of socialism in action. The Covey's inability to recognise the fact that he is really surrounded by practising socialists is one of the most effective ironies in the play.

Nationalism

O'Casey again presents us with two conflicting images in order to reveal the hollow rhetoric of fervent nationalists. Reference has already been made to the contrast between Pearse's speech and the characters' petty squabbling during Act II (see page 6). Similarly we have the boasting and posturing of Uncle Peter and Fluther, both of whom claim to have dedicated themselves to nationalism, contrasted with their subsequent actions of looting and then retreating to Bessie's attic room, when the fighting does break out.

Heroism

But there is also the more serious ironic contrast between the heroism of the rebels and that of the civilians. Jack Clitheroe is presented as a man of vanity rather than ideals. O'Casey suggests that Clitheroe's death is wasteful because the ideals behind the rising are misplaced. The same, however, cannot be said of Bessie's death, which is depicted as truly courageous. While Brennan deserts Clitheroe, leaving him to die in the burning building, we learn of Nora's brave search for her husband, and of Fluther's daring journey through the streets. O'Casey seems to be saying that these single acts of unselfish courage are more worthy than the egocentric, militarist actions of the rebels.

It could be argued that O'Casey is being unfair to those who took part in the rising. Warfare of any description is undesirable, and O'Casey is right to question the motives behind the rising of 1916. However, to suggest that so many men lost their lives simply for vanity is not really satisfactory. Too many questions are left unanswered or simply ignored. Seen from the point of view of the tenement people, the *Plough* is a superbly damning account of the rising and the whole romantic dynamism that generated it, but was the rising really a mistake in principle, and not in timing? Was it wrong to try to convince people that they should never forget their national identity, that it would be wrong to abandon the quest for a united Ireland?

Religion

Religion is seen as a powerful moral force in the day-to-day lives of these tenement characters. Without being saintly, their behaviour is affected by a set of religious values. In certain situations these values may be temporarily forgotten or reinterpreted, as in the looting scenes, but never for very long. Much of the play's irony comes from this two-faced ability to state and break the rules at the same time.

They are a God-fearing people. Uncle Peter never tires of referring to the final day of judgment; Mrs. Gogan cannot bring herself to look at a picture of *The Sleeping Venus*; Fluther fears it's a sin just to listen to The Covey. They also place a great deal of trust in God. At moments of extremity, whether painful or joyous, they turn to their God. Witness Nora's 'God be thanked' speech when Jack returns briefly, or Bessie's dying prayer, confirmation of her absolute faith:

> I do believe, I will believe
> That Jesus died for me;
> That on th' cross He shed His blood,
> From sin to set me free . . .

The subject of religion is not dealt with as a theme in its own right. It enters into the play only in so far as it is an important feature in the personalities of the characters. It is seen as a necessary but relative thing in their lives. It is a source of hope and comfort, of courage and reason, amidst the absurd chaos. It is one of the few things on which they can always rely since they have made it their own.

Romance versus Reality

This particular conflict is to be found on different levels. The setting and characters are from a real period in history and a real place. In so far as it is possible, it attempts to give us an actual true-to-life picture. And yet the *Plough* is peopled by characters who are guided by romantic aspirations rather than firm facts.

The figure speaking to the crowd outside the pub in Act II gives a romantic image of war. Nora escapes into a romantic landscape of meadows and birdsong when the pain becomes unbearable. The Covey dreams of the socialist Utopia. Each character has his or her own dreams which, in a sense, help to combat the dreariness and pain of their own futile existence. Again, a great deal of irony is derived from this conflict. Overall, O'Casey implies that we need personal dreams and colourful imaginations, but that these, taken to extreme, and imposed on others, can prove dangerous.

CONCLUSIONS

An introduction such as this can only touch on a limited number of features either of the characters or the play as a whole. Indeed, O'Casey's greatness as a playwright can to a large degree be attributed to the fact that his plays allow for no single exhaustive interpretation. We have examined the more obvious aspects of the principal characters with a view to highlighting some of the possible avenues by which they may be approached. There are more. There are two characters I have purposely not discussed: Mollser and Rosie. Are they important characters? Why are they in the play in the first place? We have looked at a brief outline of the history of the period; was it as simple as that, or are there other factors worth considering and which might shed more light on our appreciation of the play's treatment of the period? And finally, what can we say of O'Casey's philosophy or political point of view?

Above all these considerations, one thing must be kept in mind while reading the play. It was written to be performed on a stage, and therefore it is rarely the case that one person is talking and nothing else is happening. The stage is as much a visual medium as it is verbal.

O'Casey fully appreciated this fact, and *The Plough and the Stars* is filled with frantic energy and activity, all of which contribute equally to the play's ultimate effect, which is firstly to entertain, and secondly to stimulate thought.

Dublin slums around 1916

THE PLOUGH AND THE STARS

A tragedy in four acts
by
SEAN O'CASEY

CHARACTERS

Jack Clitheroe (a bricklayer), Commandant in the
  Irish Citizen Army
Nora Clitheroe, his wife
Peter Flynn (a labourer), Nora's uncle
The Young Covey (a fitter), Clitheroe's cousin
Bessie Burgess (a street fruit-vendor)
Mrs. Gogan (a charwoman)
Mollser, her consumptive child
Fluther Good (a carpenter)

*Residents
in the
Tenement*

Lieut. Langon (a Civil Servant), of the Irish Volunteers
Capt. Brennan (a chicken butcher), of the
  Irish Citizen Army
Corporal Stoddart, of the Wiltshires
Sergeant Tinley, of the Wiltshires
Rosie Redmond, a daughter of "the Digs"
A Bar-tender
A Woman
The Figure in the Window

Act I.—The living-room of the Clitheroe flat in a Dublin tenement.
Act II.—A public-house, outside of which a meeting is being held.
Act III.—The street outside the Clitheroe tenement.
Act IV.—The room of Bessie Burgess.

Time.—Acts I and II, November 1915; Acts III and IV, Easter Week,
1916. A few days elapse between Acts III and IV.

The photographs which accompany the text are by Fergus Bourke, from the Abbey Theatre's Golden Jubilee production in 1976.

Cast

Commandant Jack Clitheroe	Clive Geraghty
Nora Clitheroe	Sorcha Cusack
Peter Flynn	Bill Foley
The Young Covey	John Kavanagh
Fluther Good	Cyril Cusack
Bessie Burgess	Siobhán McKenna
Mrs. Gogan	Angela Newman
Mollser	Bernadette Shortt
Captain Brennan	Desmond Cave
Lieut. Langon	Bryan Murray
Rosie Redmond	Máire O'Neill
A Barman	Geoffrey Golden
A Woman from Rathmines	Kathleen Barrington
The Figure	Edward Golden
Sergeant Tinley	Philip O'Flynn
Corporal Stoddart	Niall O'Brien
Crowd for meeting	Philip O'Sullivan
	Stephen Brennan
	Michael O'Sullivan
	Ingrid Craigie
	Fiona Mac Anna

Director: Tomás Mac Anna

COMMENTARY ON ACT I

SUMMARY

The setting is the home of the Clitheroes: Nora and her husband Jack; Nora's uncle, Peter Flynn; and Jack's cousin, The Covey. We quickly learn from the inquisitive Mrs. Gogan that all is not well between Nora and Jack. Nora does not want Jack to continue his activities with the Citizen Army, and indeed it seems he has lost interest in the army of late: probably because he has not received word of his promotion to commandant, which he has been expecting.

Fluther and The Covey argue over politics, science and religion. The Covey taunts the risible Peter Flynn. Then Bessie Burgess enters, and attacks Nora. Things eventually settle down with The Covey's and Peter Flynn's departure to a political rally in Parnell Square. Captain Brennan arrives on the scene, and we learn that Nora has been concealing the news of her husband's promotion. She argues with Jack, who then leaves in order to take part in a mock attack on Dublin Castle. Nora is left weeping with Mrs. Gogan's daughter Mollser. War in the home, in the form of constant arguments; war on the streets, in the form of a brewing rebellion; the First World War raging on the continent—O'Casey allows Mollser to sum up Act I: 'Is there anybody goin', Mrs. Clitheroe, with a titther o' sense?'

CHARACTERS

Each of the characters is well defined in this first act. The talkative Mrs. Gogan likes to dwell a great deal on the subject of death; Fluther is seen to be both comical and good-hearted; Peter is little more than a cantankerous old fool; The Covey delivers some of the most important lines in the act, especially concerning the Citizen Army flag, but his knowledge of science and politics leave a lot to be desired; Bessie displays a frightening capacity for violence. Nora at first gives the impression of being complete master of the house, and handles Peter and The Covey confidently; however, this seems to change when Jack refuses to stay with her. Jack Clitheroe seems to be more attracted to the pomp and glory of war than anything else: he rejoins the Citizen Army only after he learns of his promotion.

STRUCTURE

This act has a very fluid structure. Although it is really made up of several small scenes, each of these flows from one to the other in rapid succession, so that we hardly notice the change. A new argument generally signifies a new scene. We go from Fluther shouting at Mrs.

Gogan, to The Covey and Fluther shouting at each other, and on to The Covey and Peter shouting at one another. Nora then finds herself confronted by Bessie. Finally Nora and Jack begin a shouting match.

LANGUAGE

It is worth noting that although the language is generally *lyrical*, it becomes more so, and less *realistic*, when people lose their tempers. For example, notice Fluther's lines:

> ... complicated cunundhrums of mollycewels an' atoms (324)
> Shoutin's no manifestin' forth of a growin' mind (333–4)

and how *alliteration* is used (words beginning with identical sounds):

> ... to stand silent and simple listening (376)
> ... makin' a maddenin' mockery o' God Almighty (377–8)

Peter gives us many such examples, particularly because he is angry most of the time:

> as stiff with starch as a shinin' band o' solid steel.

Finally we should also take note of Bessie's use of biblical phraseology. For example her last speech is really a paraphrase of the First Psalm: 'Thou shalt not be afraid for the terror by night; nor for the arrow that flieth by day; nor for the pestilence that walketh in darkness; nor for the destruction that wasteth at noonday.'

ACT I

The home of the Clitheroes. *It consists of the front
and back drawing-rooms in a fine old Georgian house,
struggling for its life against the assaults of time, and
the more savage assaults of the tenants. The room
shown is the back drawing-room, wide, spacious, and
lofty. At back is the entrance to the front drawing-room.
The space, originally occupied by folding doors, is now
draped with casement cloth of a dark purple, decorated
with a design in reddish-purple and cream. One of the
curtains is pulled aside, giving a glimpse of front
drawing-room, at the end of which can be seen the wide,
lofty windows looking out into the street. The room
directly in front of the audience is furnished in a way
that suggests an attempt towards a finer expression of
domestic life. The large fireplace on right is of wood,
painted to look like marble (the original has been taken
away by the landlord). On the mantelshelf are two
candlesticks of dark carved wood. Between them is a
small clock. Over the clock is hanging a calendar which
displays a picture of 'The Sleeping Venus'. In the centre
of the breast of the chimney hangs a picture of Robert
Emmet. On the right of the entrance to the front
drawing-room is a copy of 'The Gleaners', on the
opposite side a copy of 'The Angelus'. Underneath 'The
Gleaners' is a chest of drawers on which stands a green
bowl filled with scarlet dahlias and white chrysan-
themums. Near to the fireplace is a settee which at night
forms a double bed for* Clitheroe *and* Nora. *Underneath
'The Angelus' are a number of shelves containing sauce-
pans and a frying-pan. Under these is a table on which
are various articles of delf ware. Near the end of the
room, opposite to the fireplace, is a gate-legged table,
covered with a cloth. On top of the table a huge cavalry
sword is lying. To the right is a door which leads to a
lobby from which the staircase leads to the hall. The
floor is covered with a dark green linoleum. The room
is dim except where it is illuminated from the glow of
the fire. Through the window of the room at back can
be seen the flaring of the flame of a gasolene lamp
giving light to workmen repairing the street. Occasion-
ally can be heard the clang of crowbars striking the setts.*

2

6

8

20

22

24

32

36

41

(2) Georgian house: one of the
large terrace houses built in
Dublin in the eighteenth
century during the reigns of
Kings George I–IV of
England. (See note to line 136
below.)

(6) lofty: of imposing height.

(8) casement cloth: a type of
heavy curtain material.

(20) 'The Sleeping Venus': the
Roman goddess of love,
beauty, grace and fertility,
painted by Giorgio Barbarelli
or Giorgio da Castelfranco
(1478-1510). The picture is
that of a reclining female
nude figure.

(22) Robert Emmet (1778-1803):
United Irishman, tried by
court-martial and hanged for
leading the 1803 rising in
which he attempted to seize
Dublin Castle and capture
the viceroy.

(24) 'The Gleaners'; 'The
Angelus': pictures by Jean
François Millet (1814-75)
who became popular as a
result of his scenes of country
life.

(32) gate-legged table: a table with
legs in a gate-like frame
swinging back to allow the
top to fold down.

(36) linoleum: a floor-covering of
canvas thickly coated with
hardened linseed oil;
commonly referred to as
'lino'.

(41) setts: granite paving-blocks.

41

Fluther Good *is repairing the lock of door, Right. A claw-hammer is on a chair beside him, and he has a screw-driver in his hand. He is a man of forty years of age, rarely surrendering to thoughts of anxiety, fond of his 'oil' but determined to conquer the habit before he dies. He is square-jawed and harshly featured; under the left eye is a scar, and his nose is bent from a smashing blow received in a fistic battle long ago. He is bald, save for a few peeping tufts of reddish hair around his ears; and his upper lip is hidden by a scrubby red moustache, embroidered here and there with a grey hair. He is dressed in a seedy black suit, cotton shirt with a soft collar, and wears a very respectable little black bow. On his head is a faded jerry hat, which, when he is excited, he has a habit of knocking farther back on his head, in a series of taps. In an argument he usually fills with sound and fury generally signifiying a row. He is in his shirt-sleeves at present, and wears a soiled white apron, from a pocket in which sticks a carpenter's two-foot rule. He has just finished the job of putting on a new lock, and, filled with satisfaction, he is opening and shutting the door, enjoying the completion of a work well done. Sitting at the fire, airing a white shirt, is* Peter Flynn. *He is a little, thin bit of a man, with a face shaped like a lozenge; on his cheeks and under his chin is a straggling wiry beard of a dirty-white and lemon hue. His face invariably wears a look of animated anguish, mixed with irritated defiance, as if everybody was at war with him, and he at war with everybody. He is cocking his head in a way that suggests resentment at the presence of* Fluther, *who pays no attention to him, apparently, but is really furtively watching him.* Peter *is clad in a singlet, white whipcord knee-breeches, and is in his stocking-feet.*

A voice is heard speaking outside of door, Left (it is that of Mrs. Gogan*).*

Mrs. Gogan (*outside*). Who are you lookin' for, sir? Who? Mrs. Clitheroe? . . . Oh, excuse me. Oh ay, up this way. She's out, I think: I seen her goin'. Oh, you've somethin' for her; oh, excuse me. You're from Arnott's. . . . I see. . . . You've a parcel for her. . . . Righto. . . . I'll take it.

(46) *fond of his 'oil': he drinks more than he should.*

(55) *jerry hat: a narrow-brimmed hat then commonly worn.*

(58) *sound and fury: a reference to the famous speech in Shakespeare's* Macbeth: *'. . . It is a tale told by an idiot, full of sound and fury, signifying nothing.'*

(66) *lozenge: a rhombus or diamond-shaped figure.*

(73) *furtively: secretly or slyly.*

(81) *Arnott's: a fashionable department store in Dublin.*

. . . I'll give it to her the minute she comes in. . . . It'll be quite safe. . . . Oh, sign that. . . . Excuse me. . . . Where? . . . Here? . . . No, there; righto. Am I to put Maggie or Mrs.? What is it? You dunno? Oh, excuse me.

> [Mrs. Gogan *opens the door and comes in. She is a doleful-looking little woman of forty, insinuating manner and sallow complexion. She is fidgety and nervous, terribly talkative, has a habit of taking up things that may be near her and fiddling with them while she is speaking. Her heart is aflame with curiosity, and a fly could not come into nor go out of the house without her knowing. She has a draper's parcel in her hand, the knot of the twine tying it is untied.* Peter, *more resentful of this intrusion than of* Fluther's *presence, gets up from the chair, and without looking around, his head carried at an angry cock, marches into the room at back.*]

Mrs. Gogan (*removing the paper and opening the cardboard box it contains*). I wondher what's this now? A hat! (*She takes out a hat, black, with decorations in red and gold.*) God, she's goin' to th' divil lately for style! That hat, now, cost more than a penny. Such notions of upperosity she's gettin'. (*Putting the hat on her head*) Oh, swank, what! [*She replaces it in parcel.*] (107) (108)

Fluther. She's a pretty little Judy, all the same. (109)

Mrs. Gogan. Ah, she is, an' she isn't. There's prettiness an' prettiness in it. I'm always sayin' that her skirts are a little too short for a married woman. An' to see her, sometimes of an evenin', in her glad-neck gown would make a body's blood run cold. I do be ashamed of me life before her husband. An' th' way she thries to be polite, with her 'Good mornin', Mrs. Gogan', when she's goin' down, an' her 'Good evenin', Mrs. Gogan', when she's comin' up. But there's politeness an' politeness in it. (110) (111) (113) (114) (117)

Fluther. They seem to get on well together, all th' same.

(107) *upperosity: expensive tastes.*
(108) *swank: stylish.*
(109) *Judy: a slang term for a woman.*
(110) *she is, an' she isn't: in some respects she is and in others she is not.*
(111) *There's prettiness an' prettiness in it: there are different ways of being pretty.*
(113) *glad-neck gown: a low-cut dress.*
(114) *make a body's blood run cold: horrify a person.*
(117) *goin' down: going downstairs.*

Mrs. Gogan. Ah, they do, an' they don't. The pair o' them used to be like two turtle doves always billin' an' cooin'. You couldn't come into th' room but you'd feel, instinctive like, that they'd just been afther kissin' an' cuddlin' each other. . . . It often made me shiver, for, afther all, there's kissin' an' cuddlin' in it. But I'm thinkin' he's beginnin' to take things more quietly; the mystery of havin' a woman's a mystery no longer. . . . She dhresses herself to keep him with her, but it's no use—afther a month or two, th' wondher of a woman wears off.

Fluther. I dunno, I dunno. Not wishin' to say anything derogatory, I think it's all a question of location: when a man finds th' wondher of one woman beginnin' to die, it's usually beginnin' to live in another.

Mrs. Gogan. She's always grumblin' about havin' to live in a tenement house. 'I wouldn't like to spend me last hour in one, let alone live me life in a tenement,' says she. 'Vaults,' says she, 'that are hidin' th' dead, instead of homes that are sheltherin' th' livin'.' 'Many a good one,' says I, 'was reared in a tenement house.' Oh, you know, she's a well-up little lassie, too; able to make a shillin' go where another would have to spend a pound. She's wipin' th' eyes of th' Covey an' poor oul' Pether—everybody knows that—screwin' every penny she can out o' them, in ordher to turn th' place into a babby-house. An' she has th' life frightened out o' them; washin' their face, combin' their hair, wipin' their feet, brushin' their clothes, thrimmin' their nails, cleanin' their teeth—God Almighty, you'd think th' poor men were undhergoin' penal servitude.

Fluther (*with an exclamation of disgust*). A-a-ah, that's goin' beyond th' beyonds in a tenement house. That's a little bit too derogatory.

[Peter *enters from room, Back, head elevated and resentful fire in his eyes; he is still in his singlet and trousers, but is now wearing a pair of unlaced boots—possibly to be decent in the presence of* Mrs. Gogan. *He places the white shirt, which he has*

---

(121) billin' an' cooin': soft murmuring sounds made by doves; referring here to Nora and Clitheroe's amorous behaviour.

(132) derogatory: insulting; Fluther's favourite all-purpose word.

(136) tenement house: a large house now divided into one-room flats; the tenement houses became the slums of Dublin, disease-ridden, filthy and decayed.

(139) Vaults . . . the livin': an accurate description of the tenements at a time when Dublin reputedly had the second-highest death rate in Europe.

(139) good one: a respectable person.

(141) well up: very clever.

(142) make a shillin' go . . . a pound: manage with very little money (Nora is thrifty).

(143) wipin' th' eyes: fooling or swindling a person.

(144) screwin' every penny: taking a lot of their money (Peter and The Covey would be paying her rent).

(146) babby-house: a doll's house—tidy, clean and ordered.

(150) penal servitude: imprisonment with compulsory labour.

(152) goin' beyond th' beyonds: going too far.

carried in on his arm, on the back of a chair near the fire, and, going over to the chest of drawers, he opens drawer after drawer, looking for something; as he fails to find it he closes each drawer with a snap; he pulls out pieces of linen neatly folded, and bundles them back again any way.

Peter (*in accents of anguish*). Well, God Almighty, give me patience!

> [*He returns to room, Back, giving the shirt a vicious turn as he passes.*

Mrs. Gogan. I wondher what he is foostherin' for now? 169

Fluther. He's adornin' himself for th' meeting to-night. 170 (*Pulling a handbill from his pocket and reading*) 'Great Demonstration an' torchlight procession around places 172 in th' city sacred to th' memory of Irish Patriots, to be 173 concluded be a meetin', at which will be taken an oath of fealty to th' Irish Republic. Formation in Parnell 175 Square at eight o'clock.' Well, they can hold it for Fluther. I'm up th' pole; no more dhrink for Fluther. 177 It's three days now since I touched a dhrop, an' I feel a new man already.

Mrs. Gogan. Isn't oul' Peter a funny-lookin' little man? . . . Like somethin' you'd pick off a Christmas Tree. . . . When he's dhressed up in his canonicals, you'd 182 wondher where he'd been got. God forgive me, when I 183 see him in them, I always think he must ha' had a Mormon for a father! He an' th' Covey can't abide each 185 other; th' pair o' them is always at it, thryin' to best each other. There'll be blood dhrawn one o' these days. 187

Fluther. How is it that Clitheroe himself, now, doesn't have anythin' to do with th' Citizen Army? A couple o' 189 months ago, an' you'd hardly ever see him without his gun, an' th' Red Hand o' Liberty Hall in his hat. 191

Mrs. Gogan. Just because he wasn't made a Captain of. He 192 wasn't goin' to be in anything where he couldn't be conspishuous. He was so cocksure o' being made one 194 that he bought a Sam Browne belt, an' was always 195

---

(169) foostherin': fussing; actively doing nothing.

(170) adornin' himself: dressing himself in the gaudy green costume of the Foresters, a harmless patriotic organisation.

(170) for th' meeting: It is during this meeting that Act II takes place.

(172) Great Demonstration: calculated to stir up emotions, demonstrations such as this helped to gather momentum during the months leading up to the Rising.

(173) sacred to th' memory of Irish Patriots: in some way connected with heroic figures of the past, such as birth places and places of execution.

(175) oath of fealty: a promise of allegiance to the republican cause.

(177) up th' pole: off the drink.

(182) canonicals: a clergyman's dress or, sarcastically, an elaborate uniform.

(183) where he'd been got: where he was born; a common Dublin expression.

(185) Mormon: a member of an American sect, the Church of Jesus Christ of Latter-Day Saints, founded in 1830.

(187) to best each other: to outsmart one another.

(187) there'll be blood dhrawn: the two will come to blows.

(For notes on lines 189–195, see page 46.)

puttin' it on an' standin' at th' door showing it off, till th' man came an' put out th' street lamps on him. God, I 197 think he used to bring it to bed with him! But I'm tellin' you herself was delighted that that cock didn't crow, for 199 she's like a clockin' hen if he leaves her sight for a 200 minute.

> [*While she is talking, she takes up book after book from the table, looks into each of them in a near-sighted way, and then leaves them back. She now lifts up the sword, and proceeds to examine it.*]

Mrs. Gogan. Be th' look of it, this must ha' been a general's sword. . . . All th' gold lace an' th' fine figaries 208 on it. . . . Sure it's twiced too big for him.

Fluther. A-ah; it's a baby's rattle he ought to have, an' he 210 as he is with thoughts tossin' in his head of what may happen to him on th' day o' judgement.

> [Peter *has entered, and seeing* Mrs. Gogan *with the sword, goes over to her, pulls it resentfully out of her hands, and marches into the room, Back, without speaking.*]

Mrs. Gogan (*as* Peter *whips the sword*). Oh, excuse me! . . . (*To* Fluther) Isn't he th' surly oul' rascal!

Fluther. Take no notice of him. . . . You'd think he was dumb, but when you get his goat, or he has a few jars 220 up, he's vice versa. [*He coughs.* 221

Mrs. Gogan (*she has now sidled over as far as the shirt hanging on the chair*). Oh, you've got a cold on you, Fluther.

Fluther (*carelessly*). Ah, it's only a little one.

Mrs. Gogan. You'd want to be careful, all th' same. I knew a woman, a big lump of a woman, red-faced an' round-bodied, a little awkward on her feet; you'd think, to look at her, she could put out her two arms an' lift a two-storied house on th' top of her head; got a ticklin' in her

(189) *Citizen Army: During the 1913 strike the Dublin Metropolitan Police and hired thugs used violence against the strikers. As a result of this the Irish Citizen Army was founded by Jim Larkin and James Connolly. As we see later in the play, the army gradually became involved in the struggle for independence.*

(191) *Red Hand o' Liberty Hall: The red hand was the badge of the Irish Transport and General Workers' Union and of the Irish Citizen Army; both organisations had their headquarters in Liberty Hall.*

(192) *made a Captain of: promoted to captain.*

(194) *conspishuous [conspicuous]: as a captain, Clitheroe would be a more noticeable figure.*

(195) *Sam Browne belt: an officer's gun belt with supporting strap.*

(197) *street lamps: paraffin lamps that had to be manually turned on and off.*

(199) *that cock didn't crow: that morning did not come—Clitheroe was not promoted.*

(200) *clockin' hen: a hen with eggs—an over-anxious person.*

(208) *th' fine figaries: the filigree or decoration on Peter's sword.*

(210) *it's a baby's rattle he ought to have: he's only a child playing with toys.*

(For notes on lines 220 and 221, see page 48.)

Fluther (to Mrs. Gogan)
  'A-ah; it's a baby's rattle he ought to have . . .'
  (Act I, line 210)

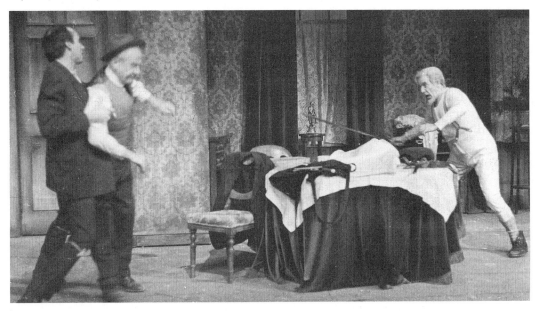

The Covey (left) with Fluther and Peter (right)
  'It's a nice thing to have a lunatic like this lashin' around with a lethal weapon!'
  (Act I, lines 430-2)

throat, an' a little cough, an' th' next mornin' she had a little catchin' in her chest, an' they had just time to wet her lips with a little rum, an' off she went. 233

[*She begins to look at and handle the shirt.*

Fluther (*a little nervously*). It's only a little cold I have; there's nothing derogatory wrong with me.

Mrs. Gogan. I dunno; there's many a man this minute lowerin' a pint, thinkin' of a woman, or pickin' out a 238 winner, or doin' work as you're doin', while th' hearse 239 dhrawn be th' horses with the black plumes is dhrivin' 240 up to his own hall door, an' a voice that he doesn't hear 241 is mutterin' in his ear, 'Earth to earth, an' ashes t' ashes, an' dust to dust.' 243

Fluther (*faintly*). A man in th' pink o' health should have 244 a holy horror of allowin' thoughts o' death to be festerin' in his mind, for (*with a frightened cough*) be 246 God, I think I'm afther gettin' a little catch in me chest that time—it's a creepy thing to be thinkin' about.

Mrs. Gogan. It is, an' it isn't; it's both bad an' good. . . . It always gives meself a kind o' threspassin' joy to feel 250 meself movin' along in a mournin' coach, an' me thinkin' that, maybe, th' next funeral 'll be me own, an' glad, in a quiet way, that this is somebody else's.

Fluther. An' a curious kind of a gaspin' for breath—I hope there's nothin' derogatory wrong with me.

Mrs. Gogan (*examining the shirt*). Frills on it, like a woman's petticoat.

Fluther. Suddenly gettin' hot, an' then, just as suddenly, gettin' cold.

Mrs. Gogan (*holding out the shirt towards* Fluther). How would you like to be wearin' this Lord Mayor's nightdhress, Fluther?

Fluther (*vehemently*). Blast you an' your nightshirt! Is a

(220) *when you get his goat: when you annoy him.*
has a few jars up: has taken a few drinks.
(221) *vice versa: the other way around; another all-purpose phrase used by Fluther.*
(233) *off she went: she died.*
(238) *lowerin' a pint: drinking a pint of stout.*
(239) *pickin' out a winner: picking a horse to bet on.*
(240) *hearse dhrawn be the horses with the black plumes: At that time a hearse would have been a carriage pulled by horses, their heads decorated with black plumes.*
(241) *a voice that he doesn't hear: the voice of Death.*
(243) *earth to earth . . . dust to dust: a paraphrase of the funeral service.*
(244) *in th' pink o' health: in perfect health.*
(246) *festerin' in his mind: building up in his mind, and infecting it like a wound.*
(250) *threspassin' joy: Joy is not something we should feel at a funeral, hence the adjective threspassin'.*

man fermentin' with fear to stick th' showin' off to him 264
of a thing that looks like a shinin' shroud? 265

Mrs. Gogan. Oh, excuse me!
> [Peter *has again entered, and he pulls the shirt
> from the hands of* Mrs. Gogan, *replacing it on
> the chair. He returns to room.*

Peter (*as he goes out*). Well, God Almighty, give me
patience!

Mrs. Gogan (*to* Peter). Oh, excuse me!
> [*There is heard a cheer from the men working
> outside on the street, followed by the clang of
> tools being thrown down, then silence. The
> glare of the gasolene light diminishes and
> finally goes out.*

Mrs. Gogan (*running into the back room to look out of
the window*). What's the men repairin' th' streets
cheerin' for?

Fluther (*sitting down weakly on a chair*). You can't sneeze
but that oul' one wants to know th' why an' th'
wherefore.... I feel as dizzy as bedamned! I hope I didn't 283
give up th' beer too suddenly.
> [The Covey *comes in by the door, Right. He is
> about twenty-five, tall, thin, with lines on his
> face that form a perpetual protest against life as
> he conceives it to be. Heavy seams fall from
> each side of nose, down around his lips, as if
> they were suspenders keeping his mouth from
> falling. He speaks in a slow, wailing drawl;
> more rapidly when he is excited. He is dressed
> in dungarees, and is wearing a vividly red tie.
> He flings his cap with a gesture of disgust on
> the table, and begins to take off his overalls.*

Mrs. Gogan (*to* The Covey, *as she runs back into the
room*). What's after happenin', Covey?

The Covey (*with contempt*). Th' job's stopped. They've

---

(264) *fermentin' with fear: being
overcome by fear.*
(264) *to stick: to put up with.*
(265) *a shinin' shroud: a white
shroud or burial dress.*
(283) *wants to know th' why an' th'
wherefore: wants to know
everything.*

been mobilized to march in th' demonstration to-night undher th' Plough an' th' Stars. Didn't you hear them cheerin', th' mugs! They have to renew their political baptismal vows to be faithful in seculo seculorum. 300 301 302

Fluther (*forgetting his fear in his indignation*). There's no reason to bring religion into it. I think we ought to have as great a regard for religion as we can, so as to keep it out of as many things as possible.

The Covey (*pausing in the taking off of his dungarees*). Oh, you're one o' the boys that climb into religion as high as a short Mass on Sunday mornin's? I suppose you'll be singin' songs o' Sion an' songs o' Tara at th' meetin', too. 308 310

Fluther. We're all Irishmen, anyhow; aren't we?

The Covey (*with hand outstretched, and in a professional tone*). Look here, comrade, there's no such thing as an Irishman, or an Englishman, or a German or a Turk; we're all only human bein's. Scientifically speakin', it's all a question of the accidental gatherin' together of mollycewels an' atoms. 314 318

    [Peter *comes in with a collar in his hand. He goes over to mirror, Left, and proceeds to try to put it on.*

Fluther. Mollycewels an' atoms! D'ye think I'm goin' to listen to you thryin' to juggle Fluther's mind with complicated cunundhrums of mollycewels an' atoms? 323 324

The Covey (*rather loudly*). There's nothin' complicated in it. There's no fear o' the Church tellin' you that mollycewels is a stickin' together of millions of atoms o' sodium, carbon, potassium o' iodide, etcetera, that, accordin' to th' way they're mixed, make a flower, a fish, a star that you see shinin' in th' sky, or a man with a big brain like me, or a man with a little brain like you!

Fluther (*more loudly still*). There's no necessity to be

(300) *th' Plough an' th' Stars: the Citizen Army flag. (See the note to line 652 below.)*
(301) *mugs: idiots.*
(302) *renew their political baptismal vows: reassert their oaths of allegiance. (See the note to line 175 above.)*
(302) *in seculo seculorum [in saecula saeculorum]: Latin for 'for ever'.*
(308) *climb into religion: become religious once a week.*
(310) *Sion: the kingdom of Heaven in the Jewish and Christian religions.*
(310) *Tara: the hill of Tara in County Meath, the ancient assembly place of the Irish chiefs and bards.*
(314) *comrade: fellow-worker or fellow-socialist.*
(318) *mollycewels [molecules].*
(323) *juggle: confuse.*
(324) *cunundhrums [conundrums]: riddles.*

50

raisin' your voice; shoutin's no manifestin' forth of a growin' mind. 334

Peter (*struggling with his collar*). God, give me patience with this thing. . . . She makes these collars as stiff with starch as a shinin' band o' solid steel! She does it purposely to thry an' twart me. If I can't get it on th' singlet, how, in th' Name o' God, am I goin' to get it on th' shirt?

The Covey (*loudly*). There's no use o' arguin' with you; it's education you want, comrade.

Fluther. The Covey an' God made th' world, I suppose, wha'?

The Covey. When I hear some men talkin' I'm inclined to disbelieve that th' world's eight-hundhred million years old, for it's not long since th' fathers o' some o' them crawled out o' th' sheltherin' slime o' the sea. 348

Mrs. Gogan (*from room at back*). There, they're afther formin' fours, an' now they're goin' to march away. 350

Fluther (*scornfully*). Mollycewels! (*He begins to untie his apron.*) What about Adam an' Eve? 352

The Covey. Well, what about them?

Fluther (*fiercely*). What about them, you?

The Covey. Adam an' Eve! Is that as far as you've got? Are you still thinkin' there was nobody in th' world before Adam and Eve? (*Loudly*) Did you ever hear, man, of th' skeleton of th' man o' Java? 358

Peter (*casting the collar from him*). Blast it, blast it, blast it! 360

Fluther (*viciously folding his apron*). Ah, you're not goin' to be let tap your rubbidge o' thoughts into th' mind o' Fluther. 362

(334) shoutin's . . . growin' mind: having a loud voice does not mean you have a large brain.

(348) disbelieve that . . . o' th' sea: According to the theory of evolution, humankind originated in the sea and gradually evolved over millions of years; The Covey maintains that people like Fluther display such ignorance that it's hard to believe they ever evolved at all.

(350) they're goin' to march away: referring to the workers outside.

(352) Adam and Eve: The biblical story tells us that God made Adam and Eve, and does not mention molecules or evolution; Fluther believes this refutes what The Covey is saying.

(358) Did you . . . man o' Java: another reference to evolution; the fossilised remains of what was believed to be the 'missing link'—half ape, half human—were found in Java (Indonesia) in 1891.

(360) Blast it . . .: While Fluther and The Covey are shouting at each other, Peter is shouting at his collar.

(362) rubbidge [rubbish].

The Covey. You're afraid to listen to th' thruth!

Fluther. Who's afraid?

The Covey. You are!

Fluther. G'way, you wurum!   367

The Covey. Who's a worum?

Fluther. You are, or you wouldn't talk th' way you're talkin'.

The Covey. Th' oul', ignorant savage leppin' up in you, 371
when science shows you that th' head of your god is an
empty one. Well, I hope you're enjoyin' th' blessin' o' 373
havin' to live be th' sweat of your brow. 374

Fluther. You'll be kickin' an' yellin' for th' priest yet, me
boyo. I'm not goin' to stand silent an' simple listenin' to
a thick like you makin' a maddenin' mockery o' God
Almighty. It 'ud be a nice derogatory thing on me
conscience, an' me dyin', to look back in rememberin'
shame of talkin' to a word-weavin' little ignorant yahoo 380
of a red flag Socialist!

Mrs. Gogan (*she has returned to the front room, and has
wandered around looking at things in general, and is
now in front of the fireplace looking at the picture
hanging over it*). For God's sake, Fluther, dhrop it;
there's always th' makin's of a row in th' mention of
religion . . . (*Looking at picture*) God bless us, it's a
naked woman! 388

Fluther (*coming over to look at it*). What's undher it?
(*Reading*) 'Georgina: The Sleepin' Vennis'. Oh, that's a
terrible picture; oh, that's a shockin' picture! Oh, th'
one that got that taken, she must have been a prime
lassie! 393

Peter (*who also has come over to look, laughing, with his

---

(367) wurum [*worm*].

(371) savage leppin' up in you:
another reference to Fluther's
forebears—the ape in him
comes to life when he is
angry.

*(373) science shows . . . an empty
one:* The Covey believes that
science proves God cannot
exist.

(374) I hope . . . your brow: He is
being sarcastic here, asking
why it is God makes men
work so hard in order to
survive.

(380) yahoo: a braggart or a
trouble-maker.

(388) a naked woman!: She is
looking at the painting of
The Sleeping Venus; *not
accustomed to classical
paintings of nudes, she finds
it embarrassing.*

(393) a prime lassie: Although
Fluther describes the picture
as 'shockin'' and 'terrible', he
comments on how agreeable
the model's figure must have
been.

body bent at the waist, and his head slightly tilted back). Hee, hee, hee, hee, hee!

Fluther (*indignantly, to* Peter). What are you hee, hee-in' for? That's a nice thing to be hee, hee-in' at. Where's your morality, man?

Mrs. Gogan. God forgive us, it's not right to be lookin' at it.

Fluther. It's nearly a derogatory thing to be in th' room where it is.

Mrs. Gogan (*giggling hysterically*). I couldn't stop any longer in th' same room with three men, afther lookin' at it!   [*She goes out.*
        [The Covey, *who has divested himself of his dungarees, throws them with a contemptuous motion on top of* Peter's *white shirt.*

Peter (*plaintively*). Where are you throwin' them? Are you thryin' to twart an' torment me again?   411

The Covey. Who's thryin' to twart you?

Peter (*flinging the dungarees violently on the floor*). You're not goin' to make me lose me temper, me young Covey.

The Covey (*flinging the white shirt on the floor*). If you're Nora's pet, aself, you're not goin' to get your way in everything.

Peter (*plaintively, with his eyes looking up at the ceiling*). I'll say nothin'. . . . I'll leave you to th' day when th' all-pitiful, all-merciful, all-lovin' God 'll be handin' you to th' angels to be rievin' an' roastin' you, tearin' 422 an' tormentin' you, burnin' an' blastin' you!

The Covey. Aren't you th' little malignant oul' bastard, 424 you lemon-whiskered oul' swine! 425

(411) *twart [thwart]: frustrate.*
(422) *rievin' [reefing]: tearing asunder.*
(424) *malignant: harmful, evil.*
(425) *lemon-whiskered: referring to Peter's beard which we are told is a 'dirty-white and lemon hue'.*

[Peter *runs to the sword, draws it, and makes for* The Covey, *who dodges him around the table;* Peter *has no intention of striking, but* The Covey *wants to take no chance.*

The Covey (*dodging*). Fluther, hold him, there. It's a nice thing to have a lunatic like this lashin' around with a lethal weapon!
[The Covey *darts out of the room, Right, slamming the door in the face of* Peter.

Peter (*battering and pulling at the door*). Lemme out, lemme out; isn't it a poor thing for a man who wouldn't say a word against his greatest enemy to have to listen to that Covey's twartin' animosities, shovin' poor, patient 438 people into a lashin' out of curses that darken his soul with th' shadow of th' wrath of th' last day!

Fluther. Why d'ye take notice of him? If he seen you didn't, he'd say nothin' derogatory.

Peter. I'll make him stop his laughin' an' leerin', jibin' an' 443 jeerin' an' scarifyin' people with his corner-boy insinuations! . . . He's always thryin' to rouse me: if it's not a song, it's a whistle; if it isn't a whistle, it's a cough. But you can taunt an' taunt—I'm laughin' at you; he, hee, hee, hee, hee, heee!

The Covey (*singing through the keyhole*):

> Dear harp o' me counthry, in darkness I
>   found thee,
> The dark chain of silence had hung o'er thee
>   long— 453

Peter (*frantically*). Jasus, d'ye hear that? D'ye hear him soundin' forth his divil-souled song o' provocation?

The Covey (*singing as before*):

> When proudly, me own island harp,
>   I unbound thee,

(438) *twártin' animosities: referring to The Covey's insults.*
(443) *jibin': mocking or taunting.*
(453) *Dear harp . . . o'er thee long: the kind of patriotic song the Foresters would sing.*

An' gave all thy chords to light, freedom an'
song!

Peter (*battering at door*). When I get out I'll do for you, I'll 461
do for you, I'll do for you!

The Covey (*through the keyhole*). Cuckoo-oo!
[Nora *enters by door, Right. She is a young
woman of twenty-two, alert, swift, full of
nervous energy, and a little anxious to get on in
the world. The firm lines of her face are con-
siderably opposed by a soft, amorous mouth
and gentle eyes. When her firmness fails her,
she persuades with her feminine charm. She is
dressed in a tailor-made costume, and wears
around her neck a silver fox fur.*

Nora (*running in and pushing* Peter *away from the door*).
Oh, can I not turn me back but th' two o' yous are at it
like a pair o' fightin' cocks! Uncle Peter . . . Uncle Peter
. . . UNCLE PETER!

Peter (*vociferously*). Oh, Uncle Peter, Uncle Peter be
damned! D'ye think I'm goin' to give a free pass to th' 478
young Covey to turn me whole life into a Holy Manual
o' penances an' martyrdoms? 480

The Covey (*angrily rushing into the room*). If you won't
exercise some sort o' conthrol over that Uncle Peter o'
yours, there'll be a funeral, an' it won't be me that'll be
in th' hearse!

Nora (*between* Peter *and* The Covey, *to* The Covey). Are
yous always goin' to be tearin' down th' little bit of
respectability that a body's thryin' to build up? Am I
always goin' to be havin' to nurse yous into th' hardy
habit o' thryin' to keep up a little bit of appearance?

The Covey. Why weren't you here to see th' way he run at
me with th' sword?

(461) *I'll do for you: a Dublin
expression meaning literally
'I'll serve time in prison for
harming you.'*
(478) *free pass: allow The Covey to
aggravate him without doing
anything to stop him.*
(480) *Holy Manual o' penances an'
martyrdoms: a misery in
which he will suffer as much
as the saintly martyrs.*

55

Peter. What did you call me a lemon-whiskered oul' swine for?

Nora. If th' two o' yous don't thry to make a generous altheration in your goin's on, an' keep on thryin' t' inaugurate th' customs o' th' rest o' th' house into this place, yous can flit into other lodgin's where your bowsey battlin' 'ill meet, maybe, with an encore.　498

Peter (*to* Nora). Would you like to be called a lemon-whiskered oul' swine?

Nora. If you attempt to wag that sword of yours at anybody again, it'll have to be taken off you an' put in a safe place away from babies that don't know th' danger o' them things.

Peter (*at entrance to room, Back*). Well, I'm not goin' to let anybody call me a lemon-whiskered oul' swine.

> [*He goes in.*

Fluther (*trying the door*). Openin' an' shuttin' now with a well-mannered motion, like a door of a select bar in a high-class pub.

Nora (*to* The Covey, *as she lays table for tea*). An', once for all, Willie, you'll have to thry to deliver yourself from　512 th' desire of provokin' oul' Pether into a wild forgetfulness of what's proper an' allowable in a respectable home.

The Covey. Well, let him mind his own business, then. Yestherday I caught him hee-hee-in' out of him an' he readin' bits out of Jenersky's *Thesis on th' Origin, Development, an' Consolidation of th' Evolutionary Idea of th' Proletariat.*　520

Nora. Now, let it end at that, for God's sake; Jack'll be in any minute, an' I'm not goin' to have th' quiet of his evenin' tossed about in an everlastin' uproar between you an' Uncle Pether. (*To* Fluther) Well, did you manage to settle th' lock, yet, Mr. Good?

(498) with an encore: with a request for more—they can go where this kind of fighting would be welcomed.

(512) deliver yourself from: control.

(520) Jenersky's Thesis . . . : the hefty title of a socialist book The Covey is reading, a parody of communist authors and their works.

Fluther (*opening and shutting door*). It's betther than a new one, now, Mrs. Clitheroe; it's almost ready to open and shut of its own accord.

Nora (*giving him a coin*). You're a whole man. How many pints will that get you?

Fluther (*seriously*). Ne'er a one at all, Mrs. Clitheroe, for Fluther's on th' wather waggon now. You could stan' where you're stannin' chantin', 'Have a glass o' malt, Fluther; Fluther, have a glass o' malt,' till th' bells would be ringin' th' ould year out an' th' New Year in, an' you'd have as much chance o' movin' Fluther as a tune on a tin whistle would move a deaf man an' he dead.

> [*As* Nora *is opening and shutting door,* Mrs. Bessie Burgess *appears at it. She is a woman of forty, vigorously built. Her face is a dogged one, hardened by toil, and a little coarsened by drink. She looks scornfully and viciously at Nora for a few moments before she speaks.*]

Bessie. Puttin' a new lock on her door . . . afraid her poor neighbours ud break through an' steal. . . . (*In a loud tone*) Maybe, now, they're a damn sight more honest than your ladyship . . . checkin' th' children playin' on th' stairs . . . gettin' on th' nerves of your ladyship. . . . Complainin' about Bessie Burgess singin' her hymns at night, when she has a few up. . . . (*She comes in half-way on the threshold, and screams*) Bessie Burgess 'll sing whenever she damn well likes!

> [Nora *tries to shut the door, but* Bessie *violently shoves it in, and, gripping* Nora *by the shoulders, shakes her.*]

Bessie. You little over-dressed throllop, you, for one pin I'd paste th' white face o' you!

Nora (*frightened*). Fluther, Fluther!

Fluther (*running over and breaking the hold of* Bessie *from* Nora). Now, now, Bessie, Bessie, leave poor Mrs.

---

(532) *on th' wather waggon:* no longer drinking.

(533) *stannin' chantin':* standing there saying.

(533) *glass o' malt:* a glass of whisky (whisky is made from malted barley).

(536) *of movin' Fluther:* of convincing me.

(548) *your ladyship:* referring to Nora and her attempts at bettering her standard of living.

(548) *checkin':* scolding the children.

(550) *singin' her hymns:* Bessie— unlike the others, who are Catholics—is a working-class Protestant, and she is in the habit, probably despite her neighbours, of singing her Protestant hymns aloud at night.

(551) *when she has a few up:* when she has been drinking.

(557) *throllop* [trollop]: an old word for 'prostitute'.

(558) *paste:* to punch a person in the face.

Clitheroe alone; she'd do no one any harm, an' minds no one's business but her own.

Bessie. Why is she always thryin' to speak proud things, 564 an' lookin' like a mighty one in th' congregation o' th' people!

> [Nora *sinks frightened on to the couch as* Jack Clitheroe *enters. He is a tall, well-made fellow of twenty-five. His face has none of the strength of* Nora's. *It is a face in which is the desire for authority, without the power to attain it.*

Clitheroe (*excitedly*). What's up? what's afther happenin'?

Fluther. Nothin', Jack. Nothin'. It's all over now. Come on, Bessie, come on.

Clitheroe (*to* Nora). What's wrong, Nora? Did she say anything to you?

Nora She was bargin' out of her, an' I only told her to 578 g'up ower o' that to her own place; an' before I knew 579 where I was, she flew at me like a tiger, an' thried to guzzle me! 581

Clitheroe (*going to door and speaking to* Bessie). Get up to your own place, Mrs. Burgess, and don't you be interferin' with my wife, or it'll be th' worse for you. . . . Go on, go on!

Bessie (*as* Clitheroe *is pushing her out*). Mind who you're pushin', now. . . . I attend me place o' worship, anyhow . . . not like some o' them that go to neither church, chapel nor meetin'-house. . . . If me son was home from th' threnches he'd see me righted. 590

> [Bessie *and* Fluther *depart, and* Clitheroe *closes the door.*

Clitheroe (*going over to* Nora, *and putting his arm round her*). There, don't mind that old bitch, Nora, darling; I'll soon put a stop to her interferin'.

(564) *to speak proud things: to boast in company.*

(578) *bargin': shouting.*

(579) *g'up ower o' that* [go up out of that].

(581) *guzzle: normally means to eat or drink quickly, but here Nora means that Bessie tried to strangle her.*

(590) *me son . . . home from the threnches: Bessie's son is away fighting in the trenches against the Germans.*

Bessie (centre) with Nora and Fluther
'Bessie Burgess'll sing whenever she damn well
likes!' (Act I, lines 552-3)

Clitheroe (between Peter and Nora) to The Covey (right)
'How are they bringin' disgrace on it?' (Act I, lines 647-8)

Nora. Some day or another, when I'm here be meself, she'll come in an' do somethin' desperate.

Clitheroe (*kissing her*). Oh, sorra fear of her doin' 598 anythin' desperate. I'll talk to her to-morrow when she's sober. A taste o' me mind that'll shock her into the sensibility of behavin' herself!

> [Nora *gets up and settles the table. She sees the dungarees on the floor and stands looking at them, then she turns to* The Covey, *who is reading Jenersky's 'Thesis' at the fire.*

Nora. Willie, is that th' place for your dungarees?

The Covey (*getting up and lifting them from the floor*). Ah, they won't do th' floor any harm, will they?

> [*He carries them into room, Back.*

Nora (*calling*). Uncle Peter, now, Uncle Peter; tea's ready.

> [Peter *and* The Covey *come in from room, Back; they all sit down to tea.* Peter *is in full dress of the Foresters: green coat, gold braided; white breeches, top boots, frilled shirt. He carries the slouch hat, with the white ostrich plume, and* 615 *the sword in his hands. They eat for a few moments in silence,* The Covey *furtively looking at* Peter *with scorn in his eyes.* Peter *knows it and is fidgety.*

The Covey (*provokingly*). Another cut o' bread, Uncle Peter? [Peter *maintains a dignified silence.*

Clitheroe. It's sure to be a great meetin' to-night. We ought to go, Nora. 623

Nora (*decisively*). I won't go, Jack; you can go if you wish.

The Covey. D'ye want th' sugar, Uncle Peter? [*A pause.*

Peter (*explosively*). Now, are you goin' to start your thryin' an' your twartin' again?

(598) *sorra fear: little fear.*
(615) *plume: a large ostrich feather.*
(623) *We ought to go: Jack, as Mrs. Gogan has told us, is no longer a member of the Citizen Army; there is then, no necessity for him to attend the meeting.*

Nora. Now, Uncle Peter, you mustn't be so touchy; Willie has only assed you if you wanted th' sugar.

Peter. He doesn't care a damn whether I want th' sugar or no. He's only thryin' to twart me!

Nora (*angrily, to* The Covey). Can't you let him alone, Willie? If he wants the sugar, let him stretch his hand out an' get it himself!

The Covey (*to* Peter). Now, if you want the sugar, you can stretch out your hand and get it yourself!

Clitheroe. To-night is th' first chance that Brennan has got of showing himself off since they made a Captain of him—why, God only knows. It'll be a treat to see him swankin' it at th' head of the Citizen Army carryin' th' flag of the Plough an' th' Stars. . . . (*Looking roguishly at* Nora) He was sweet on you, once, Nora?

Nora. He may have been. . . . I never liked him. I always thought he was a bit of a thick.

The Covey. They're bringin' nice disgrace on that banner now.

Clitheroe (*remonstratively*). How are they bringin' disgrace on it?

The Covey (*snappily*). Because it's a Labour flag, an' was never meant for politics. . . . What does th' design of th' field plough, bearin' on it th' stars of th' heavenly plough, mean, if it's not Communism? It's a flag that should only be used when we're buildin' th' barricades to fight for a Workers' Republic!

Peter (*with a puff of derision*). P-phuh.

The Covey (*angrily*). What are you phuhin' out o' you for? Your mind is th' mind of a mummy. (*Rising*) I better go an' get a good place to have a look at Ireland's warriors passin' by.

---

(637) Brennan: Captain Brennan of the Citizen Army, whom we meet a little later in this act.

(640) swankin' it: showing off.

(642) sweet on you: attracted to you.

(644) a bit of a thick: stupid.

(649) a Labour flag: a workers' flag.

(652) field plough . . . heavenly plough: The Citizen Army flag, designed by William Megahy, displays a field plough with the constellation of the same name superimposed on it, the former symbolising labour, the latter the ideals of communism.

(654) a Workers' Republic: a state governed by the workers, a socialist state.

(657) a mummy: an Egyptian mummy.

(659) Ireland's warriors: referring sarcastically to those people marching in the procession.

[*He goes into room, Left, and returns with his cap.*

Nora (*to* The Covey). Oh, Willie, brush your clothes before you go.

The Covey. Oh, they'll do well enough.

Nora. Go an' brush them; th' brush is in th' drawer there.
[The Covey *goes to the drawer, muttering, gets the brush, and starts to brush his clothes.*

The Covey (*singing at* Peter, *as he does so*):
Oh, where's th' slave so lowly,
Condemn'd to chains unholy,
Who, could he burst his bonds at first,
Would pine beneath them slowly?

We tread th' land that . . . bore us,
Th' green flag glitters . . . o' er us,
Th' friends we've tried are by our side,
An' th' foe we hate . . . before us!   675

Peter (*leaping to his feet in a whirl of rage*). Now, I'm tellin' you, me young Covey, once for all, that I'll not stick any longer these tittherin' taunts of yours, rovin' around to 678 sing your slights an' slandhers, reddenin' th' mind of a 679 man to th' thinkin' an' sayin' of things that sicken his soul with sin! (*Hysterical; lifting up a cup to fling at* The Covey) Be God, I'll—

Clitheroe (*catching his arm*). Now then, none o' that, none o' that!

Nora. Uncle Pether, Uncle Pether, UNCLE PETHER!

The Covey (*at the door, about to go out*). Isn't that th' malignant oul' varmint! Lookin' like th' illegitimate 687 son of an illegitimate child of a corporal in th' Mexican army!   [*He goes out.*

Peter (*plaintively*). He's afther leavin' me now in such a state of agitation that I won't be able to do meself justice when I'm marchin' to th' meetin'.

---

(675) *Oh, where's th' slave . . . :*
The origin of this song is unknown: O'Casey may well have composed it himself. It contains the kind of romantic terms that a patriotic body such as the Foresters would be familiar with. The Covey is again being sarcastic.
(678) *tittherin'* [*tittering*]*: little.*
(679) *slights: insults.*
(679) *reddenin': making a man angry.*
(687) *varmint* [*vermin*]*.*

62

Nora (*jumping up*). Oh, for God's sake, here, buckle your sword on, and go to your meetin', so that we'll have at least one hour of peace!

> [*She proceeds to belt on the sword.*

Clitheroe (*irritably*). For God's sake hurry him up ou' o' this, Nora.

Peter. Are yous all goin' to thry to start to twart me now?

Nora (*putting on his plumed hat*). S-s-sh. Now, your hat's on, your house is thatched; off you pop!

> [*She gently pushes him from her.*

Peter (*going, and turning as he reaches the door*). Now, if that young Covey—

Nora. Go on, go on. 　　　　　　　　　　[*He goes*
> [Clitheroe *sits down in the lounge, lights a cigarette, and looks thoughtfully into the fire.* Nora *takes the things from the table, placing them on the chest of drawers. There is a pause, then she swiftly comes over to him and sits beside him.*

Nora (*softly*). A penny for them, Jack!　　　　712

Clitheroe. Me? I was thinkin' of nothing.

Nora. You were thinkin' of th' . . . meetin' . . . Jack. When we were courtin' an' I wanted you to go, you'd say, 'Oh, to hell with meetin's,' an' that you felt lonely in cheerin' crowds when I was absent. An' we weren't a month married when you began that you couldn't keep away from them.

Clitheroe. Oh, that's enough about th' meetin'. It looks as if you wanted me to go th' way you're talkin'. You were always at me to give up th' Citizen Army, an' I gave it up; surely that ought to satisfy you.

Nora. Ay, you gave it up—because you got th' sulks when 724

63

(712) a penny for them [your thoughts]: what are you thinking?

(724) got th' sulks: became resentful.

they didn't make a Captain of you. It wasn't for my sake, Jack.

Clitheroe. For your sake or no, you're benefitin' by it, aren't you? I didn't forget this was your birthday, did I? (*He puts his arms around her*) And you liked your new hat; didn't you, didn't you?

> [*He kisses her rapidly several times.*

Nora (*panting*). Jack, Jack; please, Jack! I thought you were tired of that sort of thing long ago.

Clitheroe. Well, you're finding out now that I amn't tired of it yet, anyhow. Mrs. Clitheroe doesn't want to be kissed, sure she doesn't (*He kisses her again*) Little, little red-lipped Nora!

Nora (*coquettishly removing his arm from around her*). 738 Oh, yes, your little, little red-lipped Nora's a sweet little girl when th' fit seizes you; but your little, little red-lipped Nora has to clean your boots every mornin', all the same.

Clitheroe (*with a movement of irritation*). Oh, well, if we're goin' to be snotty! [*A pause.*

Nora. It's lookin' like as if it was you that was goin' to be . . . snotty! Bridlin' up with bitherness, th' minute a 746 body attempts t' open her mouth.

Clitheroe. Is it any wondher, turnin' a tendher sayin' into a meanin' o' malice an' spite! 749

Nora. It's hard for a body to be always keepin' her mind bent on makin' thoughts that'll be no longer than th' length of your own satisfaction. [*A pause.* 752

Nora (*standing up*). If we're goin' to dhribble th' time 753 away sittin' here like a pair o' cranky mummies, I'd be as well sewin' or doin' something about th' place.

> [*She looks appealingly at him for a few moments;*

(738) *coquettishly: in an enticing or loving manner.*

(746) *Bridlin' up with bitherness: showing resentment.*

(749) *turnin' . . . an' spite: twisting words around and causing them to have the opposite meaning.*

(752) *It's hard . . . satisfaction: Nora is pointing out how difficult it is to say a word without offending Jack.*

(753) *dhribble [dribble]: in dribs and drabs; wasting their time away.*

he doesn't speak. She swiftly sits down beside him, and puts her arm around his neck.

Nora (*imploringly*). Ah, Jack, don't be so cross!

Clitheroe (*doggedly*). Cross? I'm not cross; I'm not a bit cross. It was yourself started it.

Nora (*coaxingly*). I didn't mean to say anything out o' the way. You take a body up too quickly, Jack. (*In an ordinary tone as if nothing of an angry nature had been said*) You didn't offer me me evenin' allowance yet.
    [Clitheroe *silently takes out a cigarette for her and himself and lights both.*

Nora (*trying to make conversation*). How quiet th' house is now; they must be all out.

Clitheroe (*rather shortly*). I suppose so.

Nora (*rising from the seat*). I'm longin' to show you me new hat, to see what you think of it. Would you like to see it?

Clitheroe. Ah, I don't mind.
    [Nora *suppresses a sharp reply, hesitates for a moment, then gets the hat, puts it on, and stands before* Clitheroe.

Nora. Well, how does Mr. Clitheroe like me new hat?

Clitheroe. It suits you, Nora, it does right enough.
    [*He stands up, puts his hand beneath her chin, and tilts her head up. She looks at him roguishly. He bends down and kisses her.*

Nora. Here, sit down, an' don't let me hear another cross word out of you for th' rest o' the night.
                    [*They sit down.*

Clitheroe (*with his arms around her*). Little, little, red-lipped Nora!

(763) *out o' the way: to say the wrong thing.*
(763) *You take a body up too quickly: you are too quick to seize on the wrong meaning.*
(765) *me evenin' allowance: Normally referring to wages, here Nora uses the phrase in asking for a cigarette.*

Nora (*with a coaxing movement of her body towards him*). Jack!

Clitheroe (*tightening his arms around her*). Well?

Nora. You haven't sung me a song since our honeymoon. Sing me one now, do . . . please, Jack!

Clitheroe. What song? 'Since Maggie Went Away'?

Nora. Ah, no, Jack, not that; it's too sad. 'When You said You Loved Me.'

> [*Clearing his throat,* Clitheroe *thinks for a moment and then begins to sing.* Nora, *putting an arm around him, nestles her head on his breast and listens delightedly.*

Clitheroe (*singing verses following to the air of 'When You and I were Young, Maggie'*):
> Th' violets were scenting th' woods, Nora,
> 　Displaying their charm to th' bee,
> When I first said I lov'd only you, Nora,
> 　An' you said you lov'd only me!
>
> Th' chestnut blooms gleam'd through th' glade, Nora,
> 　A robin sang loud from a tree,
> When I first said I lov'd only you, Nora,
> 　An' you said you lov'd only me!
>
> Th' golden-rob'd daffodils shone, Nora,
> 　An' danc'd in th' breeze on th' lea,
> When I first said I lov'd only you, Nora,
> 　An' you said you lov'd only me!
>
> Th' trees, birds, an' bees sang a song, Nora,
> 　Of happier transports to be,
> When I first said I lov'd only you, Nora,
> 　An' you said you lov'd only me!
> 　　　　　　　　　　　　　[Nora *kisses him.*
> [*A knock is heard at the door, Right; a pause as they listen.* Nora *clings closely to* Clitheroe.

Another knock, more imperative than the first.

Clitheroe. I wonder who can that be, now?

Nora (*a little nervous*). Take no notice of it, Jack; they'll go away in a minute.
[*Another knock, followed by a voice.*

Voice. Commandant Clitheroe, Commandant Clitheroe, are you there? A message from General Jim Connolly. 828

Clitheroe. Damn it, it's Captain Brennan. 829

Nora (*anxiously*). Don't mind him, don't mind, Jack. Don't break our happiness . . . Pretend we're not in. Let us forget everything to-night but our two selves!

Clitheroe (*reassuringly*). Don't be alarmed, darling; I'll just see what he wants, an' send him about his business.

Nora (*tremulously*). No, no. Please, Jack; don't open it. Please, for your own little Nora's sake!

Clitheroe (*rising to open the door*). Now don't be silly, Nora.
[Clitheroe *opens the door, and admits a young man in the full uniform of the Irish Citizen Army—green suit; slouch green hat caught up at one side by a small Red Hand badge; Sam* 842 *Browne belt, with a revolver in the holster. He* 843 *carries a letter in his hand. When he comes in he smartly salutes* Clitheroe. *The young man is* Captain Brennan.

Capt. Brennan (*giving the letter to* Clitheroe). A dispatch 847 from General Connolly.

Clitheroe (*reading. While he is doing so,* Brennan's *eyes are fixed on* Nora, *who droops as she sits on the lounge*). 'Commandant Clitheroe is to take command of the eighth battalion of the I.C.A. which will assemble to proceed to the meeting at nine o'clock. He is to see that

(828) *Jim Connolly: James Connolly (1868–1916), one of the founders of the Irish Citizen Army, and one of the leaders of the 1916 rising.*
(829) *Brennan: already referred to slightingly by Jack.*
(842) *Red Hand badge: see the note to line 191 above.*
(843) *Sam Browne belt: see the note to line 195 above.*
(847) *dispatch: a letter containing instructions.*

all units are provided with full equipment; two days' rations and fifty rounds of ammunition. At two o'clock A.M. the army will leave Liberty Hall for a re- 856 connaissance attack on Dublin Castle.—Com.-Gen. 857 Connolly.'

Clitheroe. I don't understand this. Why does General Connolly call me Commandant?

Capt. Brennan. Th' Staff appointed you Commandant, and th' General agreed with their selection.

Clitheroe. When did this happen?

Capt. Brennan. A fortnight ago.

Clitheroe. How is it word was never sent to me?

Capt. Brennan. Word was sent to you. . . . I meself brought it.

Clitheroe. Who did you give it to, then?

Capt. Brennan (*after a pause*). I think I gave it to Mrs. Clitheroe, there.

Clitheroe. Nora, d'ye hear that? [Nora *makes no answer.*

Clitheroe (*there is a note of hardness in his voice*). Nora . . . Captain Brennan says he brought a letter to me from General Connolly, and that he gave it to you. . . . Where is it? What did you do with it?

Nora (*running over to him, and pleadingly putting her arms around him*). Jack, please, Jack, don't go out to-night an' I'll tell you; I'll explain everything. . . . Send him away, an' stay with your own little red-lipp'd Nora.

Clitheroe (*removing her arms from around him*). None o' this nonsense, now; I want to know what you did with th' letter?

(856) *Liberty Hall: see the note to line 191 above.*

(857) *reconnaissance: military examination of a region.*

(857) *attack on Dublin Castle: Mock insurrections were routinely and openly staged by the Volunteers and the Citizen Army as training exercises. The authorities chose to ignore these harmless war games; when the Easter Rising took place, it was only by degrees that people came to realise they were more than mere demonstrations. The mock attack referred to here did in fact take place at this particular time.*

[Nora *goes slowly to the lounge and sits down.*

(910) *'The Soldiers' Song': a march written in 1907 by Peadar Kearney and Patrick Heeney; now the national anthem.*

Clitheroe (*angrily*). Why didn't you give me th' letter? What did you do with it? . . . (*He shakes her by the shoulder*) What did you do with th' letter?

Nora (*flaming up*). I burned it, I burned it! That's what I did with it! Is General Connolly an' th' Citizen Army goin' to be your only care? Is your home goin' to be only a place to rest in? Am I goin' to be only somethin' to provide merry-makin' at night for you? Your vanity'll be th' ruin of you an' me yet. . . . That's what's movin' you: because they've made an officer of you, you'll make a glorious cause of what you're doin', while your little red-lipp'd Nora can go on sittin' here, makin' a companion of th' loneliness of th' night!

Clitheroe (*fiercely*). You burned it, did you? (*He grips her arm*) Well, me good lady—

Nora. Let go—you're hurtin' me!

Clitheroe. You deserve to be hurt. . . . Any letter that comes to me for th' future, take care that I get it. . . . D'ye hear—take care that I get it!
[*He goes to the chest of drawers and takes out a Sam Browne belt, which he puts on, and then puts a revolver in the holster. He puts on his hat, and looks towards* Nora. *While this dialogue is proceeding, and while* Clitheroe *prepares himself,* Brennan *softly whistles 'The Soldiers' Song'.* 910

Clitheroe (*at door, about to go out*). You needn't wait up for me; if I'm in at all, it won't be before six in th' morning.

Nora (*bitterly*). I don't care if you never come back!

Clitheroe (*to* Capt. Brennan). Come along, Ned.
[*They go out; there is a pause.* Nora *pulls her new hat from her head and with a bitter movement*

69

flings it to the other end of the room. There is a gentle knock at door, Right, which opens, and Mollser comes into the room. She is about fifteen, but looks to be only about ten, for the ravages of consumption have shrivelled her up. 922 *She is pitifully worn, walks feebly, and frequently coughs. She goes over to* Nora.

Mollser (*to* Nora). Mother's gone to th' meetin', an' I was feelin' terribly lonely, so I come down to see if you'd let me sit with you, thinkin' you mightn't be goin' yourself. . . . I do be terrible afraid I'll die sometime when I'm be meself. . . . I often envy you, Mrs. Clitheroe, seein' th' health you have, an' the lovely place you have here, an' wondherin' if I'll ever be sthrong enough to be keepin' a home together for a man. Oh, this must be some more o' the Dublin Fusiliers flyin' off to the front. 934

[*Just before* Mollser *ceases to speak, there is heard in the distance the music of a brass band playing a regiment to the boat on the way to the front. The tune that is being played is 'It's a Long Way to Tipperary'; as the band comes to the chorus, the regiment is swinging into the street by* Nora's *house, and the voices of the soldiers can be heard lustily singing the chorus of the song.*

It's a long way to Tipperary, it's a long way to go;
It's a long way to Tipperary, to th' sweetest girl I know!
Goodbye, Piccadilly; farewell Leicester Square.
It's a long, long way to Tipperary, but my heart's right there?

[Nora *and* Mollser *remain silently listening. As the chorus ends and the music is faint in the distance again,* Bessie Burgess *appears at door, Right, which* Mollser *has left open.*

Bessie (*speaking in towards the room*). There's th' men marchin' out into th' dhread dimness o' danger, while th' lice is crawlin' about feedin' on th' fatness o' the land! But yous'll not escape from th' arrow that flieth be

---

(922) *the ravages of consumption:* 'consumption' (now called tuberculosis) killed an enormous number of people in Dublin at this time, and particularly the poor. Judging by Mollser's condition, she is in the final stages of the disease.

(934) *Dublin Fusiliers:* an Irish regiment of the British army, on their way to the front in France.

night, or th' sickness that wasteth be day. . . . An' ladyship an' all, as some o' them may be, they'll be scattered abroad, like th' dust in th' darkness! 959

[Bessie *goes away;* Nora *steals over and quietly shuts the door. She comes back to the lounge and wearily throws herself on it beside* Mollser.

Mollser (*after a pause and a cough*). Is there anybody goin', Mrs. Clitheroe, with a titther o' sense? 964

CURTAIN

END ACT I

(959) *There's the men . . . like th' dust in th' darkness!: In Biblical tones, Bessie predicts ruin and destruction for those who ignore their duty and whose minds are set on treachery, their 'duty' being to fight—like her son—against the Germans and not the English.*

(964) *titther: small amount.*

COMMENTARY ON ACT II

SUMMARY

The setting of Act II is a public house, although the events in the street outside are just as much a part of this act. Very little actually takes place in this act as far as the story or narrative moving forward is concerned. Outside, the meeting spoken of in Act I is taking place. Through the large two-paned windows we see the silhouette of a man, and intermittently we hear his voice and the passionate words he uses to address the crowd. Meanwhile, all the characters we met in Act I, other than Nora and Mollser, enter and leave the pub and manage to embroil themselves in at least one argument.

But there are two main arguments. The first is between Bessie and Mrs. Gogan, with The Covey siding with Bessie, and Fluther and Peter siding with Mrs. Gogan. The two women are finally evicted from the pub, leaving Peter with Mrs. Gogan's infant in his arms. The second argument, between Fluther and The Covey, is almost a mirror image of their argument in Act I. It begins as a political argument and ends in a fist fight, Fluther proudly defending Rosie's honour. Act I ends with the sound of the Dublin Fusiliers marching to war, Act II with the sound of the Citizen Army marching to Dublin Castle.

STRUCTURE

As in Act I, we move from one argument to the next, but Act II is structurally much more complex. We are really in two places at the same time, the bar and the street. The link between these two locations is of course the figure silhouetted in the window. It becomes clear very quickly why O'Casey uses this technique. The speaker outside is a fervent idealist, but his ideals do not seem to match reality, that is, with those who are squabbling and drinking in the bar. We hear of the fight for freedom, but what we see of fighting is by no means glorious or heroic. So we get what is called *dramatic irony*, in this case the actions of the people on stage being completely at odds with what the speaker proclaims.

LANGUAGE

We could go so far as to say that this act is about language, or rather its uses and abuses. The speaker is using language to incite the crowd gathered at the meeting. He is celebrating the concept of war. It is spoken of with religious fervour. We have words such as 'glorious', 'cleansing', 'sanctifying', etc. He speaks of men shedding their blood for freedom as Jesus did for mankind. He also uses repetition as a

72

device for rousing the crowd, for example 'we must accustom ourselves', 'they think . . .' or his final lines, 'the fools, the fools. . . .' Words such as 'manhood' and 'slavery', with their overtones of shame and cowardice, are also used purposely to agitate the crowd. This is what we call *rhetoric*: but he is not the only person who uses rhetoric.

The arguments among those in the bar become verbal battles. The language becomes intensely complicated as each person tries to outwit the other with words. Notice how Bessie and Mrs. Gogan for instance begin by insulting each other as if neither one were in the pub, referring to the other person as 'some people' or 'a certain lassie'. And after The Covey has been thrown out of the bar by the barman, Fluther, who has not laid a finger on The Covey, acts victoriously. He has beaten him with words.

The Covey uses his own rhetoric in the form of socialist jargon while talking to Rosie and, before his fight, with Fluther. All in all, one of the most important features of this act is the way in which these different forms of language are charged with energy and life.

ACT II

A commodious public-house at the corner of the street ₁
in which the meeting is being addressed from Platform ₂
No. 1. It is the south corner of the public-house that is
visible to the audience. The counter, beginning at Back
about one-fourth of the width of the space shown, comes
across two-thirds of the length of the stage, and, taking a
circular sweep, passes out of sight to Left. On the
counter are beer-pulls, glasses, and a carafe. The other ₈
three-fourths of the Back is occupied by a tall, wide,
two-paned window. Beside this window at the Right is ₁₀
a small, box-like, panelled snug. Next to the snug is a ₁₁
double swing door, the entrance to that particular end
of the house. Farther on is a shelf on which customers
may rest their drinks. Underneath the windows is a
cushioned seat. Behind the counter at Back can be seen
the shelves running the whole length of the counter. On
these shelves can be seen the end (or the beginning) of
rows of bottles. The Barman *is seen wiping the part of*
the counter which is in view. Rosie *is standing at the*
counter toying with what remains of a half of whisky in ₂₀
a wine-glass. She is a sturdy, well-shaped girl of twenty, ₂₁
pretty, and pert in manner. She is wearing a cream ₂₂
blouse, with an obviously suggestive glad neck; a grey ₂₃
tweed dress, brown stockings and shoes. The blouse and
most of the dress are hidden by a black shawl. She has no
hat, and in her hair is jauntily set a cheap, glittering,
jewelled ornament. It is an hour later. ₂₇

Barman (*wiping counter*). Nothin' much doin' in your
line to-night, Rosie? ₂₉

Rosie. Curse o' God on th' haporth, hardly, Tom. There ₃₀
isn't much notice taken of a pretty petticoat of a night ₃₁
like this. . . . They're all in a holy mood. Th' solemn-
lookin' dials on th' whole o' them an' they marchin' to ₃₃
th' meetin'. You'd think they were th' glorious
company of th' saints, an' th' noble army of martyrs
thrampin' through th' streets of paradise. They're all
thinkin' of higher things than a girl's garthers. . . . It's a ₃₇
tremendous meetin'; four platforms they have—there's

74

(1) commodious: with plenty of room.
(2) the meeting: this is the same meeting talked of in Act I. (See Act I, line 172.)
(8) beer-pulls: as the name suggests, large handles used for pulling draught beer.
(8) carafe: a decorative glass bottle for water or wine.
(10) wide, two-paned window: The window needs to be large enough for the full-sized shadow of a man to be seen through it.
(11) panelled snug: a small compartment that allowed customers to drink in privacy if they so wished.
(20) toying with: playing with it, trying to make it last.
(21) whisky in a wine-glass: in order to give customers the impression that she is drinking a more respectable drink than whisky.
(22) pert: saucy or impudent.
(23) glad neck: a low neckline.
(27) an hour later: Only one hour has passed since Act I. Act III, on the other hand, occurs several months after Act II.
(29) in your line: Rosie, as The Covey later blurts out, is a prostitute, a common feature of Dublin night-life then.
(30) haporth [halfpenny-worth]: a negligible amount.
(31) pretty petticoat: referring to herself.
(33) dials: faces.
(37) higher things: a reference to the high ideals of the marchers.
(37) garthers [garters]: bands worn above the knees to keep up stockings.

one o' them just outside opposite th' window.

Barman. Oh, ay; sure when th' speaker comes (*motioning with his hand*) to th' near end, here, you can see him plain, an' hear nearly everythin' he's spoutin' out of him. 42

Rosie. It's no joke thryin' to make up fifty-five shillin's a 44 week for your keep an' laundhry, an' then taxin' you a 45 quid for your own room if you bring home a friend for th' night. . . . If I could only put by a couple of quid for a swankier outfit, everythin' in th' garden ud look lovely— 48

Barman. Whisht, till we hear what he's sayin'. 49
[*Through the window is silhouetted the figure of a tall man who is speaking to the crowd. The* Barman *and* Rosie *look out of the window and listen.*

The Voice of the Man. It is a glorious thing to see arms in 54 the hands of Irishmen. We must accustom ourselves to the thought of arms, we must accustom ourselves to the sight of arms, we must accustom ourselves to the use of arms. . . . Bloodshed is a cleansing and sanctifying thing, and the nation that regards it as the final horror has lost its manhood. . . . There are many things more horrible than bloodshed, and slavery is one of them!
[*The figure moves away towards the Right, and is lost to sight and hearing.*

Rosie. It's th' sacred thruth, mind you, what that man's afther sayin'.

Barman. If I was only a little younger, I'd be plungin' mad 66 into th' middle of it!

Rosie (*who is still looking out of the window*). Oh, here's the two gems runnin' over again for their oil! 69
[Peter *and* Fluther *enter tumultuously. They are* 70 *hot, and full and hasty with the things they have seen and heard. Emotion is bubbling up in them, so that when they drink, and when* 73

(42) *spoutin': shouting.*
(44) *make up: earn.*
(45) *keep an' laundhry . . . : Rosie would have lived in what was Dublin's 'red light' district: an area containing many brothels. A brothel would probably have been like a hostel in that the prostitutes would pay for their meals and the use of a single room and an extra amount for each customer—or 'friend', as Rosie calls them—they brought home.*
(48) *swankier outfit: more fashionable clothes.*
(48) *everythin' in th' garden ud look lovely: things in general would be a lot better.*
(49) *Whisht: be quiet.*
(54) *Voice of the Man: Throughout this act, the words of the orator are actually those of Patrick Pearse, and include extracts from his speech at the graveside of O'Donovan Rossa.*
(66) *plungin' mad: immersing himself in the crowd with enthusiasm.*
(69) *two gems: two gentlemen— Fluther and Peter.*
(69) *their oil: their supply of alcohol.*
(70) *tumultuously: in great excitement.*
(73) *Emotion is bubbling up in them: They are in a state of excitement as a result of the speech outside.*

they speak, they drink and speak with the fullness of emotional passion. Peter *leads the way to the counter.*

Peter (*splutteringly to* Barman). Two halves ... (*To* 77
Fluther) A meetin' like this always makes me feel as if I could dhrink Loch Erinn dhry!

Fluther. You couldn't feel any way else at a time like this when th' spirit of a man is pulsin' to be out fightin' for 81 th' thruth with his feet thremblin' on th' way, maybe to th' gallows, an' his ears tinglin' with th' faint, far-away sound of burstin' rifle-shots that'll maybe whip th' last little shock o' life out of him that's left lingerin' in his body!

Peter. I felt a burnin' lump in me throat when I heard th' band playin' 'The Soldiers' Song', rememberin' last 88 hearin' it marchin' in military formation with th' people starin' on both sides at us, carryin' with us th' pride an' resolution o' Dublin to th' grave of Wolfe Tone. 92

Fluther. Get th' Dublin men goin' an' they'll go on full force for anything that's thryin' to bar them away from 94 what they're wantin', where th' slim thinkin' counthry 95 boyo ud limp away from th' first faintest touch of compromization! 97

Peter (*hurriedly to the* Barman). Two more, Tom! ... (*To* Fluther) Th' memory of all th' things that was done, an' all th' things that was suffered be th' people, was boomin' in me brain. .... Every nerve in me body was 101 quiverin' to do somethin' desperate!

Fluther. Jammed as I was in th' crowd, I listened to th' speeches patherin' on th' people's head, like rain fallin' on th' corn; every derogatory thought went out o' me mind, an' I said to meself, 'You can die now, Fluther, for you've seen th' shadow-dhreams of th' past 107 leppin' to life in th' bodies of livin' men that show, if we 108 were without a titther o' courage for centuries, we're 109

(77) *Two halves: two small measures of whisky.*

(81) *pulsin' his pulse beating with excitement.*

(88) *'The Soldiers' Song': See the note to line 910 in Act I.*

(92) *Wolfe Tone: Theobald Wolfe Tone (1763–98), founder of the United Irishmen; condemned to death for his part in the 1798 rising.*

(94) *bar them away from: prevent them from getting.*

(95) *slim thinkin': narrow-minded.*

(97) *compromization: a made-up word meaning a confrontation that would compromise themselves and their own safety.*

(101) *boomin' in me brain: resounding through his head.*

(107) *shadow-dhreams of th' past: spirits of past ages.*

(108) *leppin' to life: Possessed by such spirits, the people are filled with courage.*

(109) *titther: See the note to line 964 in Act I.*

Fluther (to Peter, with Rosie, left)
   '. . . if we were without a titther o' courage for centuries, we're vice versa now!'
   (Act II, lines 108-10)

Bessie to Mrs. Gogan (holding baby)
   'Bessie Burgess doesn't put up to know much, never havin' a swaggerin' mind, thanks be to
   God . . .' (Act II, lines 364-5)

vice versa now!' Looka here. (*He stretches out his arm* 110 *under* Peter's *face and rolls up his sleeve*). The blood was BOILIN' in me veins!

[*The silhouette of the tall figure again moves* 113 *into the frame of the window speaking to the people.*

Peter (*unaware, in his enthusiasm, of the speaker's appearance, to* Fluther). I was burnin' to dhraw me sword, an' wave an' wave it over me—

Fluther (*overwhelming* Peter). Will you stop your blatherin' for a minute, man, an' let us hear what he's 120 sayin'!

Voice of the Man. Comrade soldiers of the Irish Volunteers 122 and of the Citizen Army, we rejoice in this terrible war. The old heart of the earth needed to be warmed with the red wine of the battlefields. . . . Such august homage 125 was never offered to God as this: the homage of millions of lives given gladly for love of country. And we must be ready to pour out the same red wine in the same glorious sacrifice, for without shedding of blood there is no 129 redemption!

[*The figure moves out of sight and hearing.*

Fluther (*gulping down the drink that remains in his glass, and rushing out*). Come on, man; this is too good to be missed!

[Peter *finishes his drink less rapidly, and as he is going out wiping his mouth with the back of his hand he runs into* The Covey *coming in. He immediately erects his body like a young cock, and with his chin thrust forward, and a look of venomous dignity on his face, he marches out.*

The Covey (*at counter*). Give us a glass o' malt, for God's 141 sake, till I stimulate meself from the shock o' seein' th' 142 sight that's afther goin' out!

Rosie (*all business, coming over to the counter, and* 144 *standing near* The Covey). Another one for me,

(110) *vice versa: See the note to line 221 in Act I.*

(113) *The silhouette: The speaker is pacing up and down on a platform. We are therefore only catching parts of his speech.*

(120) *blatherin': foolish talk.*

(122) *Irish Volunteers: Formed in 1913 soon after the formation of the Citizen Army. Many of its leaders followed the IRB's policy that British power must be overthrown by force, although officially they were committed to the defensive policy of Eoin MacNeill, their chief of staff. Pearse was director of military organisation.*

(125) *august: noble or venerable.*

(125) *homage: reverence or tribute.*

(129) *red wine . . . sacrifice: Wine here, as in line 125 above, symbolically refers to blood, using the image of Jesus's blood being sacrificed in the form of the Eucharist.*

(141) *glass o' malt: a glass of whisky.*

(142) *stimulate meself: try to recover.*

(144) *all business: Rosie sees a potential customer in* The Covey.

Tommy; (*to the* Barman) th' young gentleman's ordherin' it in th' corner of his eye.

[*The* Barman *brings the drink for* The Covey, *and leaves it on the counter.* Rosie *whips it up.*

Barman. Ay, houl' on there, houl' on there, Rosie!   150

Rosie (*to the* Barman). What are you houldin' on out o' you for? Didn't you hear th' young gentleman say that he couldn't refuse anything to a nice little bird? (*To* The   153 Covey) Isn't that right, Jiggs? (The Covey *says*   154 *nothing*). Didn't I know, Tommy, it would be all right? It takes Rosie to size a young man up, an' tell th' thoughts that are thremblin' in his mind. Isn't that right, Jiggs?

[The Covey *stirs uneasily, moves a little farther away, and pulls his cap over his eyes.*

Rosie (*moving after him*). Great meetin' that's gettin' held outside. Well, it's up to us all, anyway, to fight for our freedom.

The Covey (*to* Barman). Two more, please. (*To* Rosie) Freedom! What's th' use o' freedom, if it's not economic freedom?   166

Rosie (*emphasizing with extended arm and moving finger*). I used them very words just before you come in. 'A lot o' thricksters,' says I, 'that wouldn't know what freedom was if they got it from their mother.' . . . (*To* Barman) Didn't I, Tommy?

Barman. I disremember.   172

Rosie. No, you don't disremember. Remember you said, yourself, it was all 'only a flash in th' pan'. Well, 'flash   174 in th' pan, or no flash in th' pan,' says I, 'they're not goin' to get Rosie Redmond,' says I, 'to fight for freedom that wouldn't be worth winnin' in a raffle!'

The Covey. There's only one freedom for th' workin' man: conthrol o' th' means o' production, rates of exchange,   179

(150) houl' on [hold on].
(153) bird: a slang word for a woman.
(154) Jiggs: an arbitrary nickname.
(166) economic freedom: the right of a country to have an independent economy.
(172) I disremember: I forget.
(174) a flash in th' pan: a brief outburst, not to be taken seriously.
(179) conthrol o' th' means o' production . . . : a garbled version of the socialist demand that the state should control the production, distribution and exchange of goods.

an' th' means of disthribution. (*Tapping* Rosie *on the shoulder*) Look here, comrade, I'll leave here tomorrow night for you a copy of Jenersky's *Thesis on the Origin, Development, an' Consolidation of the Evolutionary Idea of the Proletariat.*

Rosie (*throwing off her shawl on to the counter, and showing an exemplified glad neck, which reveals a good deal of a white bosom*). If y'ass Rosie, it's heartbreakin' to see a young fella thinkin' of anything, or admirin' anything, but silk thransparent stockin's showin' off the shape of a little lassie's legs!
    [The Covey, *frightened, moves a little away.*

Rosie (*following on*). Out in th' park in th' shade of a warm summery evenin', with your little darlin' bridie 193 to be, kissin' an' cuddlin' (*she tries to put her arm around his neck*), kissin' an' cuddlin', ay?

The Covey (*frightened*). Ay, what are you doin'? None o' that, now; none o' that. I've something else to do besides shinannickin' after Judies! 198
    [*He turns away, but* Rosie *follows, keeping face to face with him.*

Rosie. Oh, little duckey, oh, shy little duckey! Never held a mot's hand, an' wouldn't know how to tittle a little 202 Judy! (*She clips him under the chin.*) Tittle him undher 203 th' chin, tittle him under th' chin!

The Covey (*breaking away and running out*). Ay, go on, now; I don't want to have any meddlin' with a lassie like you!

Rosie (*enraged*). Jasus, it's in a monasthery some of us ought to be, spendin' our holidays kneelin' on our adorers, tellin' our beads, an' knockin' hell out of our buzzums! 211

The Covey (*outside*). Cuckoo-oo!
    [Peter *and* Fluther *come in again, followd by* Mrs. Gogan, *carrying a baby in her arms. They*

(193) bridie: bride.
(198) shinannickin' after Judies: chasing after women.
(202) mot: Dublin slang for 'girl'.
(203) tittle [tickle].
(211) knockin' hell out of our buzzums [bosoms]: the penitential act of striking one's breast in prayer.

go over to the counter.

Peter (*with plaintive anger*). It's terrible that young Covey 216
can't let me pass without proddin' at me! Did you hear 217
him murmurin' 'cuckoo' when we were passin'?

Fluther (*irritably*). I wouldn't be everlastin' cockin' me ear 219
to hear every little whisper that was floatin' around
about me! It's my rule never to lose me temper till it
would be dethrimental to keep it. There's nothin' 222
derogatory in th' use o' th' word 'cuckoo', is there?

Peter (*tearfuly*). It's not th' word; it's th' way he says it: he
never says it straight out, but murmurs it with curious
quiverin' ripples, like variations on a flute!

Fluther. Ah, what odds if he gave it with variations on a 227
thrombone! (*To* Mrs. Gogan) What's yours goin' to be,
ma'am?

Mrs. Gogan. Ah, a half o' malt, Fluther. 230

Fluther (*to* Barman). Three halves, Tommy.
       [*The* Barman *brings the drinks.*

Mrs. Gogan (*drinking*). The Foresthers' is a gorgeous
dhress! I don't think I've seen nicer, mind you, in a 234
pantomime. . . . Th' loveliest part of th' dhress, I think,
is th' osthrichess plume. . . . When yous are goin' along, 236
an' I see them wavin' an' noddin' an' waggin', I seem to
be lookin' at each of yous hangin' at th' end of a rope,
your eyes bulgin' an' your legs twistin' an' jerkin',
gaspin' an' gaspin' for breath while yous are thryin' to
die for Ireland!

Fluther. If any o' them is hangin' at the end of a rope, it 242
won't be for Ireland!

Peter. Are you goin' to start th' young Covey's game o'
proddin' an' twartin' a man? There's not many that's
talkin' can say that for twenty-five years he never missed
a pilgrimage to Bodenstown! 247

(216) *plaintive:
mournful-sounding.*
(217) *proddin': provoking.*
(219) *everlastin': always.*
(219) *cockin' me ear: listening out
for.*
(222) *dethrimental: harmful.*
(227) *what odds!: so what?*
(230) *half o' malt: a small measure
of whisky.*
(234) *a gorgeous dhress: Peter's
outrageous costume.*
(236) *When yous are goin' along
. . . : The dangling feathers in
Peter's cap remind her of a
man dangling from a gallows.*
(242) *any o' them: 'them' being the
Foresters, who never involved
themselves in anything more
than colourful parades.*
(247) *pilgrimage to Bodenstown:
referring to the annual
commemorations held at
Wolfe Tone's grave in
Bodenstown, County Kildare.*

Fluther. You're always blowin' about goin' to Bodens- 248 town. D'ye think no one but yourself ever went to Bodenstown?

Peter (*plaintively*). I'm not blowin' about it; but there's not a year that I go there but I pluck a leaf off Tone's grave, an' this very day me prayer-book is nearly full of them.

Fluther (*scornfully*). Then Fluther has a vice versa opinion of them that put ivy leaves into their prayer- 256 books, scabbin' it on th' clergy, an' thryin' to out-do th' 257 haloes o' th' saints be lookin' as if he was wearin' around his head a glittherin' aroree boree allis! 259 (*Fiercely*) Sure, I don't care a damn if you slep' in Bodenstown! You can take your breakfast, dinner, an' tea on th' grave in Bodenstown, if you like, for Fluther!

Mrs. Gogan. Oh, don't start a fight, boys, for God's sake; I was only sayin' what a nice costume it is—nicer than th' kilts, for, God forgive me, I always think th' kilts is hardly decent.

Fluther. Ah, sure, when you'd look at him, you'd wondher whether th' man was makin' fun o' th' costume, or th' costume was makin' fun o' th' man!

Barman. Now, then, thry to speak asy, will yous? We don't 270 want no shoutin' here.
　　　[The Covey *followed by* Bessie Burgess *comes in. They go over to the opposite end of the counter, and direct their gaze on the other group.*

The Covey (*to* Barman). Two glasses o' malt.

Peter. There he is, now; I knew he wouldn't be long till he folleyed me in. 277

Bessie (*speaking to* The Covey, *but really at the other party*). I can't for th' life o' me undherstand how they can call themselves Catholics, when they won't lift a finger to help poor little Catholic Belgium. 281

(248) blowin': boasting.
(256) a vice versa opinion: a low opinion.
(257) scabbin': breaking a strike, or (loosely) taking another person's work. Peter is being two-faced by placing such mementoes, of a person whom the Church would not approve of, in his prayer-book.
(259) aroree boree allis [aurora borealis]: the northern lights.
(270) speak asy [speak easy]: keep your voices down.
(277) folleyed [followed].
(281) Catholic Belgium: A significant factor in motivating Irishmen to join the British army during the First World War was the fact that Belgium was a Catholic country, and the slogan 'Help little Catholic Belgium' was widely used on recruiting posters.

Mrs. Gogan (*raising her voice*). What about poor little Catholic Ireland?

Bessie (*over to* Mrs. Gogan). You mind your own business, ma'am, an' stupefy your foolishness be gettin' dhrunk. ₂₈₅

Peter (*anxiously*). Take no notice of her; pay no attention to her. She's just tormentin' herself towards havin' a row with somebody.

Bessie. There's a storm of anger tossin' in me heart, thinkin' of all th' poor Tommies, an' with them me ₂₉₀ own son, dhrenched in water an' soaked in blood, gropin' their way to a shattherin' death, in a shower o' shells! Young men with th' sunny lust o' life beamin' in them, layin' down their white bodies, shredded into torn an' bloody pieces, on th' althar that God Himself has built for th' sacrifice of heroes! ₂₉₆

Mrs. Gogan. Isn't it a nice thing to have to be listenin' to a lassie an' hangin' our heads in a dead silence, knowin' that some persons think more of a ball of malt than they ₂₉₉ do of th' blessed saints. ₃₀₀

Fluther. Whisht; she's always dangerous an' derogatory when she's well oiled. Th' safest way to hindher her from havin' any enjoyment out of her spite, is to dip our thoughts into the fact of her bein' a female person that ₃₀₄ has moved out of th' sight of ordinary sensible people. ₃₀₅

Bessie. To look at some o' th' women that's knockin' about, now, is a thing to make a body sigh. . . . A woman on her own, dhrinkin' with a bevy o' men, is ₃₀₈ hardly an example to her sex. . . . A woman dhrinkin' with a woman is one thing, an' a woman dhrinkin' with herself is still a woman—flappers may be put in another ₃₁₁ category altogether—but a middle-aged married woman makin' herself th' centre of a circle of men is as a woman that is loud an' stubborn, whose feet abideth not in her own house. ₃₁₅

The Covey (*to* Bessie). When I think of all th' problems in

(285) *stupefy your foolishness . . . : drink yourself into a stupor so that your foolishness does not show.*

(290) *Tommies: British soldiers.*

(296) *on th' althar . . . of heroes!: Bessie believes that those in Belgium are fighting a religious war and are therefore God's martyrs.*

(299) *some persons: obviously referring to Bessie.*

(299) *a ball of malt: a glass of whisky.*

(300) *th' blessed saints: Mrs. Gogan is here referring to the fact that Bessie is a Protestant.*

(304) *to dip our thoughts into: to take account of.*

(305) *has moved . . . sensible people: is not altogether sane.*

(308) *dhrinkin' with a bevy o' men: Bessie maintains that one woman in the company of a group of men is immoral.*

(311) *flappers: fashionable women of the period.*

(315) *abideth not in her own house: an example of Bessie's use of Biblical phraseology.*

front o' th' workers, it makes me sick to be lookin' at oul' codgers goin' about dhressed up like green- accoutred figures gone asthray out of a toyshop! 318 319

Peter. Gracious God, give me patience to be listenin' to that blasted young Covey proddin' at me from over at th' other end of th' shop!

Mrs. Gogan (*dipping her finger in the whisky, and moistening with it the lips of her baby*). Cissie Gogan's a woman livin' for nigh on twenty-five years in her own 325 room, an' beyond biddin' th' time o' day to her 326 neighbours, never yet as much as nodded her head in th' direction of other people's business, while she knows some as are never content unless they're standin' senthry over other people's doin's! 330

[*Bessie is about to reply, when the tall, dark figure is again silhouetted against the window, and the voice of the speaker is heard speaking passionately.*

Voice of Speaker. The last sixteen months have been the 335 most glorious in the history of Europe. Heroism has come back to the earth. War is a terrible thing, but war is not an evil thing. People in Ireland dread war because they do not know it. Ireland has not known the exhilaration of war for over a hundred years. When war comes to Ireland she must welcome it as she would welcome the Angel of God!

[*The figure passes out of sight and hearing.*

The Covey (*towards all present*). Dope, dope. There's 344 only one war worth havin': th' war for th' economic emancipation of th' proletariat. 346

Bessie. They may crow away out o' them; but it ud be 347 fitther for some o' them to mend their ways, an' cease 348 from havin' scouts out watchin' for th' comin' of th' Saint Vincent de Paul man, for fear they'd be nailed 350 lowerin' a pint of beer, mockin' th' man with an angel face, shinin' with th' glamour of deceit an' lies! 352

(318) codgers: fools.
(319) accoutred: attired or costumed.
(319) gone asthray out of a toyshop: like a mislaid toy soldier.
(325) nigh on: nearly.
(326) beyond: other than.
(330) standin' senthry . . . : always watching what other people are doing.
(335) sixteen months: the length of time the war has been raging on the continent.
(344) dope: misleading information.
(346) th' proletariat: the working class.
(347) they: referring to Mrs. Gogan.
(347) crow away: talk and boast to their heart's content.
(348) but it ud be fitther . . . : Bessie is saying that Mrs. Gogan spends the money given to her by the Saint Vincent de Paul Society on drink, and for this reason she is in constant fear of being seen in a pub.
(350) nailed: caught in the act.
(352) with an angel face . . . deceit an' lies: Bessie alleges that Mrs. Gogan puts on an angelic face to deceive the Saint Vincent de Paul man.

Mrs. Gogan. An' a certain lassie standin' stiff behind her own door with her ears cocked listenin' to what's being said, stuffed till she's sthrained with envy of a neighbour thryin' for a few little things that may be got be hard sthrivin' to keep up to th' letther an' th' law, an' th' practices of th' Church!

353
354
355
356

358

Peter (*to* Mrs. Gogan). If I was you, Mrs. Gogan, I'd parry her jabbin' remarks be a powerful silence that'll keep her tantalizin' words from penethratin' into your feelin's. It's always betther to leave these people to th' vengeance o' God!

Bessie. Bessie Burgess doesn't put up to know much, never havin' a swaggerin' mind, thanks be to God, but goin' on packin' up knowledge accordin' to her conscience: precept upon precept, line upon line; here a little, an' there a little. But (*with a passionate swing of her shawl*), thanks be to Christ, she knows when she was got, where she was got, an' how she was got; while there's some she knows, decoratin' their finger with a well-polished weddin' ring, would be hard put to it if they were assed to show their weddin' lines!

364
365

368

373

Mrs. Gogan (*plunging out into the centre of the floor in a wild tempest of hysterical rage*). Y' oul' rip of a blasted liar, me weddin' ring's been well earned be twenty years be th' side o' me husband, now takin' his rest in heaven, married to me be Father Dempsey, in th' Chapel o' Saint Jude's, in th' Christmas Week of eighteen hundhred an' ninety-five; an' any kid, livin' or dead, that Jinnie Gogan's had since, was got between th' bordhers of th' Ten Commandments! . . . An' that's more than some o' you can say that are kep' from th' dhread o' desthruction be a few drowsy virtues, that th' first whisper of temptation lulls into a sleep, that'll know one sin from another only on th' day of their last anointin', an' that use th' innocent light o' th' shinin' stars to dip into th' sins of a night's diversion!

377

382
383
384
385

388

Bessie (*jumping out to face* Mrs. Gogan, *and bringing the palms of her hands together in sharp claps to emphasize*

---

(353) *An' a certain lassie: Bessie.*

(354) *standin' stiff behind her own door: standing hidden behind her door.*

(354) *ears cocked: ears raised in listening, as a dog's might be.*

(355) *stuffed till she's sthrained with envy: filled with envy.*

(356) *a neighbour: Mrs. Gogan may be referring to herself or to Nora.*

(356) *thryin' for a few little things: Again, this may be a reference to things Nora has furnished her home with, such as the pictures and flowers.*

(358) *letther an' . . . th' Church: Bearing in mind that Bessie also attacked Nora because she does not attend church, it would seem that Mrs. Gogan is here defending Nora. She points out that acting according to the exact dictates of the church is not always easy when times are so difficult.*

(364) *put up to know much: pretend to be knowledgeable.*

(365) *havin' a swaggerin' mind: showing off.*

(368) *packin' up knowledge . . . a little: she has learned what she knows little by little, one thing at a time.*

(373) *But . . . weddin' lines: Bessie implies that Mrs. Gogan has had a number of children out of wedlock.*

(For notes on lines 377-388, see page 86.)

her remarks). Liar to you, too, ma'am, y' oul' hardened threspasser on other people's good nature, wizenin' up 392 your soul in th' arts o' dodgeries, till every dhrop of respectability in a female is dhried up in her, lookin' at your ready-made manoeuverin' with th' menkind! 395

Barman. Here, there; here, there; speak asy there. No rowin' here, no rowin' here, now.

Fluther (*trying to calm* Mrs. Gogan). Now Jinnie, Jinnie, it's a derogatory thing to be smirchin' a night like this with a row; it's rompin' with th' feelin's of hope we ought to be, instead o' bein' vice versa!

Peter (*trying to quiet* Bessie). I'm terrible dawny, Mrs. 402 Burgess, an' a fight leaves me weak for a long time aftherwards. . . . Please, Mrs. Burgess, before there's damage done, try to have a little respect for yourself.

Bessie (*with a push of her hand that sends* Peter *tottering to the end of the shop*). G'way, you little sermonizing, little yella-faced, little consequential, little pudgy, little bum, you!

Mrs. Gogan (*screaming*). Fluther, leggo! I'm not goin' to 410 keep an unresistin' silence, an' her scattherin' her festherin' words in me face, stirrin' up every dhrop of 412 decency in a respectable female, with her restless rally o' lies that would make a saint say his prayer backwards!

Bessie (*shouting*). Ah, everybody knows well that th' best charity that can be shown to you is to hide th' thruth as much as our thrue worship of God Almighty will allow us!

Mrs. Gogan (*frantically*). Here, houl' th' kid, one o' yous; 419 houl' th' kid for a minute! There's nothin' for it but to show this lassie a lesson or two. . . . (*To* Peter) Here, houl' th' kid, you. (*Before* Peter *is aware of it, she places the infant in his arms.*)

Mrs. Gogan (*to* Bessie, *standing before her in a fighting*

---

(377) me husband, now takin' his rest in heaven: It seems, if we calculate twenty years from 1895, that Mrs. Gogan is a widow of one year. This would also be consistent with the age of her infant who is about one year old.

(382) between th' bordhers of th' Ten Commandments: She has broken none of the Commandments.

(383) kep' from th' dhread o' desthruction: from fear of being condemned to hell.

(384) a few drowsy virtues: a few half-hearted morals.

(385) lulls into a sleep: At the first sign of temptation these morals are instantly disregarded.

(388) diversion: entertainment or pastime; she does not say what exactly it is Bessie gets up to on such nights.

(392) hardened threspasser . . .: slanderer of people's good character.

(392) wizenin' up: shrivelling up.

(395) ready-made . . . menkind: referring to her flirtations with men.

(402) dawny: poorly, unwell.

(410) leggo [let go].

(412) scattherin' her festherin' words: spreading vicious rumours.

(419) houl' th' kid: During all this commotion Mrs. Gogan has had the infant in her arms.

attitude). Come on, now, me loyal lassie, dyin' with grief for little Catholic Belgium! When Jinnie Gogan's done with you, you'll have a little leisure lyin' down to think an' pray for your king an' counthry!

Barman (*coming from behind the counter, getting between the women, and proceeding to push them towards the door*). Here, now, since yous can't have a little friendly argument quietly, you'll get out o' this place in quick time. Go on, an' settle your differences somewhere else—I don't want to have another endorsement on me licence.

Peter (*anxiously, over to* Mrs. Gogan). Here, take your kid back, ower this. How nicely I was picked, now, for it to be plumped into me arms!

The Covey. She knew who she was givin' it to, maybe.

Peter (*hotly to* The Covey). Now, I'm givin' you fair warnin', me young Covey, to quit firin' your jibes an' jeers at me. . . . For one o' these days, I'll run out in front o' God Almighty an' take your sacred life!

Barman (*pushing* Bessie *out after* Mrs. Gogan). Go on, now; out you go.

Bessie (*as she goes out*). If you think, me lassie, that Bessie Burgess has an untidy conscience, she'll soon show you to th' differ!

Peter (*leaving the baby down on the floor*). Ay, be Jasus, wait there, till I give her back her youngster! (*He runs to the door.*) Ay, there, ay! (*He comes back.*) There, she's afther goin' without her kid. What are we goin' to do with it, now?

The Covey. What are we goin' to do with it? Bring it outside an' show everybody what you're afther findin'!

Peter (*in a panic to* Fluther). Pick it up, you, Fluther, an' run afther her with it, will you?

(427) *leisure lyin' down: that is, after Mrs. Gogan has knocked her to the floor.*
(428) *king and counthry: England and the English king.*
(435) *another endorsement: another offence listed on his pub licence.*
(437) *ower this [out of this].*
(448) *show you to th' differ: show it is not so.*

Fluther. What d'ye take Fluther for? You must think Fluther's a right gom. D'ye think Fluther's like your- self, destitute of a titther of undherstandin'? 459 460

Barman (*imperatively to* Peter). Take it up, man, an' run out afther her with it, before she's gone too far. You're not goin' to leave th' bloody thing here, are you?

Peter (*plaintively, as he lifts up the baby*). Well, God Almighty, give me patience with all th' scorners, tor- mentors, an' twarters that are always an' ever thryin' to goad me into prayin' for their blindin' an' blastin' an' burnin' in th' world to come! [*He goes out.* 466 467 468

Fluther. God, it's a relief to get rid o' that crowd. Women is terrible when they start to fight. There's no holdin' them back. (*To* The Covey) Are you goin' to have anything?

The Covey. Ah, I don't mind if I have another half.

Fluther (*to* Barman). Two more, Tommy, me son.
[*The* Barman *gets the drinks.*

Fluther. You know, there's no conthrollin' a woman when she loses her head. 477
[Rosie *enters and goes over to the counter on the side nearest to* Fluther.

Rosie (*to* Barman). Divil a use i' havin' a thrim little leg on a night like this; things was never worse. . . . Give us a half till to-morrow, Tom, duckey. 480

Barman (*coldly*). No more to-night, Rosie; you owe me for three already.

Rosie (*combatively*). You'll be paid, won't you?

Barman. I hope so.

Rosie. You hope so! Is that th' way with you, now?

(459) gom [*Irish* gam]: *a fool.*
(460) destitute of a titther of undherstandin': *without any understanding.*
(466) twarters [thwarters]: *tormentors.*
(467) goad: *torment or incite.*
(468) prayin' . . . to come: *praying that they burn in hell.*
(477) loses her head: *becomes angry.*
(480) Divil a use: *it's no use.*
(480) thrim [trim]: *shapely.*

Fluther (*to* Barman). Give her one; it'll be all right.

Rosie (*clapping* Fluther *on the back*). Oul' sport!

Fluther. Th' meetin' should be soon over, now.

The Covey. Th' sooner th' betther. It's all a lot o' blasted nonsense, comrade.

Fluther. Oh, I wouldn't say it was all nonsense. Afther all, Fluther can remember th' time, an' him only a dawny chiseulur, bein' taught at his mother's knee to be faithful to th' Shan Van Vok! 495 496

The Covey. That's all dope, comrade; th' sort o' thing that workers are fed on be th' Boorzwawzee. 498

Fluther (*a little sharply*). What's all dope? Though I'm sayin' it that shouldn't: (*catching his cheek with his hand, and pulling down the flesh from the eye*) d'ye see that mark there, undher me eye? . . . A sabre slice from a dragoon in O'Connell Street! (*Thrusting his head forward towards* Rosie) Feel that dint in th' middle o' me nut! 500 503 505

Rosie (*rubbing* Fluther's *head, and winking at* The Covey). My God, there's a holla!

Fluther (*putting on his hat with quiet pride*). A skelp from a bobby's baton at a Labour meetin' in th' Phoenix Park! 508

The Covey. He must ha' hitten you in mistake. I don't know what you ever done for th' Labour movement. 511

Fluther (*loudly*). D'ye not? Maybe, then, I done as much, an' know as much about th' Labour movement as th' chancers that are blowin' about it! 515

Barman. Speak easy, Fluther, thry to speak easy.

The Covey. There's no necessity to get excited about it,

---

(495) *chiselur: Dublin slang for a child, perhaps derived from the old plural* childer.

(496) *Shan Van Vok* [Seanbhean Bhocht]: *the Poor Old Woman—a symbol of Ireland in distress.*

(498) *Boorzwawzee* [bourgeoisie]: *the capitalist class.*

(500) *Though I'm sayin' it that shouldn't: modesty should prevent him from showing off his wounds like this.*

(503) *A sabre slice from a dragoon: a wound caused by the sword of a mounted infantryman.*

(505) *dint in th' middle o' me nut: a hollow in his skull.*

(508) *skelp* [Irish sceilp]: *a blow.*

(511) *ha' hitten: have hit.*

(515) *chancers: frauds—referring to* The Covey.

comrade.

Fluther (*more loudly*). Excited? Who's gettin' excited? There's no one gettin' excited! It would take something more than a thing like you to flutther a feather o' Fluther. Blatherin', an', when all is said, you know as much as th' rest in th' wind up! 521 522 523

The Covey. Well, let us put it to th' test, then, an' see what you know about th' Labour movement: what's the mechanism of exchange? 526

Fluther (*roaring, because he feels he is beaten*). How th' hell do I know what it is? There's nothin' about that in th' rules of our Thrades Union!

Barman. For God's sake, thry to speak easy, Fluther.

The Covey. What does Karl Marx say about th' Relation of Value to th' Cost o' Production? 531 532

Fluther (*angrily*). What th' hell do I care what he says? I'm Irishman enough not to lose me head be follyin' foreigners! 535

Barman. Speak easy, Fluther.

The Covey. It's only waste o' time talkin' to you, comrade.

Fluther. Don't be comradin' me, mate. I'd be on me last legs if I wanted you for a comrade. 539

Rosie (*to* The Covey). It seems a highly rediculous thing to hear a thing that's only an inch or two away from a kid, swingin' heavy words about he doesn't know th' meanin' of, an' uppishly thryin' to down a man like Misther Fluther here, that's well flavoured in th' knowledge of th' world he's livin in. 542 543 544

The Covey (*savagely to* Rosie). Nobody's askin' you to be buttin' in with your prate.... I have you well taped, me lassie.... Just you keep your opinions for your own 547

(521) *flutther a feather o'Fluther: disturb Fluther.*
(522) *Blatherin': see the note to line 120 above.*
(523) *th' wind up: in the end.*
(526) *mechanism of exchange: the money system.*
(531) *Karl Marx (1818–83): German socialist philosopher; in his theories of political economy he attacked the capitalist system and advocated class warfare to abolish it.*
(532) *Relation of Value to th' Cost o' Production: the relationship of the price of an article to the expenses incurred in its production.*
(535) *follyin' foreigners: referring to Marx's being a German.*
(539) *on me last legs: in a state of desperation.*
(542) *swingin' heavy words: using large complicated words.*
(543) *uppishly: arrogantly.*
(544) *well flavoured in . . . : with plenty of experience of.*
(547) *buttin' in with your prate: interrupting with your talk.*
(547) *I have you well taped: I know what you're up to.*

Fluther to The Covey
'Maybe, then, I done as much, an' know as much, about th' Labour movement as th' chancers that are blowin' about it!' (Act II, lines 513-5)

Rosie to The Covey (seated)
'If I was a man, or you were a woman, I'd bate th' puss o' you!' (Act II, lines 557-8)

place. . . . It'll be a long time before Th' Covey takes any insthructions or reprimandin' from a prostitute!

Rosie (*wild with humiliation*). You louse, you louse, you! . . . You're no man. . . . You're no man . . . I'm a woman, anyhow, an' if I'm a prostitute aself, I have me feelin's. . . . Thryin' to put his arm around me a minute ago, an' givin' me th' glad eye, th' little wrigglin' lump o' 555 desolation turns on me now, because he saw there was nothin' doin'. . . . You louse, you! If I was a man, or you 557 were a woman, I'd bate th' puss o' you! 558

Barman. Ay, Rosie, ay! You'll have to shut your mouth altogether, if you can't learn to speak easy!

Fluther (*to* Rosie). Houl' on there, Rosie; houl' on there. There's no necessity to flutther yourself when you're with Fluther. . . . Any lady that's in th' company of Fluther is goin' to get a fair hunt. . . . This is outside 564 your province. . . . I'm not goin' to let you demean 565 yourself be talkin' to a tittherin' chancer. . . . Leave this to Fluther—this is a man's job. (*To* The Covey) Now, if you've anything to say, say it to Fluther, an', let me tell you, you're not goin' to be pass-remarkable to any lady 569 in my company.

The Covey. Sure I don't care if you were runnin' all night afther your Mary o' th' Curlin' Hair, but, when you 572 start tellin' luscious lies about what you done for th' 573 Labour movement, it's nearly time to show y'up! 574

Fluther (*fiercely*). Is it you show Fluther up? G'way, man, I'd beat two o' you before me breakfast!

The Covey (*contemptuously*). Tell us where you bury your dead, will you? 578

Fluther (*with his face stuck into the face of* The Covey). Sing a little less on th' high note, or, when I'm done 580 with you, you'll put a Christianable consthruction on 581 things, I'm tellin' you!

(555) *th' glad eye: amorous glances.*
(557) *nothin' doin': she was not interested in him.*
(558) *bate th' puss o' you: beat the face of you.*
(564) *fair hunt: will be treated properly, given a fair chance.*
(565) *outside your province: does not concern you.*
(569) *pass-remarkable: insulting.*
(572) *Mary o' th' Curlin' Hair: from a popular song of the period.*
(573) *luscious lies: big lies.*
(574) *show y' up: show you for what you really are.*
(578) *Tell us where you bury your dead: since you've killed so many people, where is it you bury them?*
(580) *th' high note: stop speaking in such a lofty tone.*
(581) *put a Christianable consthruction: speak in more polite terms to people; show more respect.*

The Covey. You're a big fella, you are.

Fluther (*tapping* The Covey *threateningly on the shoulder*). Now, you're temptin' Providence when you're temptin' Fluther! ₅₈₅

The Covey (*losing his temper, and bawling*). Easy with them hands, there, easy with them hands! You're startin' to take a little risk when you commence to paw ₅₈₉ The Covey.

    [Fluther *suddenly springs into the middle of the shop, flings his hat into the corner, whips off his coat, and begins to paw the air.*

Fluther (*roaring at the top of his voice*). Come on, come on, you lowser; put your mits up now, if there's a man's ₅₉₅ blood in you! Be God, in a few minutes you'll see some snots flyin' around, I'm tellin' you. . . . When Fluther's ₅₉₇ done with you, you'll have a vice versa opinion of him! Come on, now, come on!

Barman (*running from behind the counter and catching hold of* The Covey). Here, out you go, me little bowsey. ₆₀₁ Because you got a couple o' halves you think you can act as you like. (*He pushes* The Covey *to the door*) Fluther's a friend o' mine, an' I'll not have him insulted.

The Covey (*struggling with the* Barman). Ay, leggo, leggo there; fair hunt, give a man a fair hunt! One minute with him is all I ask; one minute alone with him, while you're runnin' for th' priest an' th' doctor.

Fluther (*to the* Barman). Let him go, let him go, Tom! let him open th' door to sudden death if he wants to!

Barman (*to* The Covey). Go on, out you go an' do th' bowsey somewhere else.

    [He pushes The Covey out and comes back.

Rosie (*getting* Fluther's *hat as he is putting on his coat*). Be God, you put th' fear o' God in his heart that time! I thought you'd have to be dug out of him. . . . Th' way ₆₁₆

(585) *Providence: in this context, fate.*
(589) *paw: to touch him with his fists.*
(595) *lowser [louser]: a low or despicable person.*
(595) *mits [mitts]: fists.*
(597) *snots flyin' around: Presumably the impact of fists on noses will cause runny 'snots' or nasal mucus.*
(601) *bowsey: a bully.*
(616) *dug out of him: taken out of The Covey as if he were a bullet.*

93

you lepped out without any of your fancy side-steppin'! 617
'Men like Fluther,' says I to meself, 'is gettin' scarce
nowadays.'

Fluther (*with proud complacency*). I wasn't goin' to let
meself be malignified by a chancer. . . . He got a little bit 621
too derogatory for Fluther. . . . Be God, to think of a cur 622
like that comin' to talk to a man like me!

Rosie (*fixing on his hat*). Did j'ever! 624

Fluther. He's lucky he got off safe. I hit a man last week,
Rosie, an' he's fallin' yet! 626

Rosie. Sure, you'd ha' broken him in two if you'd ha'
hitten him one clatther! 628

Fluther (*amorously, putting his arm around* Rosie). Come
on into th' snug, me little darlin', an' we'll have a few
dhrinks before I see you home. 631

Rosie. Oh, Fluther, I'm afraid you're a terrible man for th'
women.
    [*They go into the snug as* Clitheroe, Captain 634
    Brennan, *and* Lieut. Langon *of the Irish Volun-*
    teers enter hurriedly. Captain Brennan *carries*
    the banner of The Plough and the Stars, *and*
    Lieut. Langon *a green, white, and orange Tri-*
    colour. They are in a state of emotional
    excitement. Their faces are flushed and their
    eyes sparkle; they speak rapidly, as if unaware
    of the meaning of what they said. They have
    been mesmerized by the fervency of the
    speeches. 644

Clitheroe (*almost pantingly*). Three glasses o' port!
    [*The* Barman *brings the drinks.*

Capt. Brennan. We won't have long to wait now.

Lieut. Langon. Th' time is rotten ripe for revolution. 648

---

(617) *side-steppin': hesitating or
dallying.*

(621) *malignified by a chancer:
maligned or insulted by a
fraud.*

(622) *cur: a worthless or cowardly
person.*

(624) *Did j'ever!: did you ever hear
of such a thing!*

(626) *fallin' yet: The man he
supposedly hit is still falling.*

(628) *clatther [clatter]: a blow.*

(631) *Come on . . . see you home:
Rosie's compliments have
had the desired effect: she has
found herself a customer.*

(634) *snug: See the note to line 11
above.*

(644) *mesmerized by the fervency of
the speeches: put into a
trance-like state by the force
of the orator's words.*

(648) *rotten ripe: more than ready,
over-ripe.*

94

The Covey (left)
  'One minute with him is all I ask; one minute alone . . .' (Act II, lines 606-7)

Clitheroe with Langon (left) and Brennan (right)
  'Death for th' Independence of Ireland!' (Act II, line 670)

Clitheroe. You have a mother, Langon.

Lieut. Langon. Ireland is greater than a mother.

Capt. Brennan. You have a wife, Clitheroe.

Clitheroe. Ireland is greater than a wife.

Lieut. Langon. Th' time for Ireland's battle is now—th' place for Ireland's battle is here.
> [*The tall, dark figure again is silhouetted against the window. The three men pause and listen.*

Voice of the Man. Our foes are strong, but strong as they are, they cannot undo the miracles of God, who ripens in the heart of young men the seeds sown by the young men of a former generation. They think they have pacified Ireland; think they have foreseen everything; think they have provided against everything; but the fools, the fools, the fools!—they have left us our Fenian dead, and, while Ireland holds these graves, Ireland, unfree, shall never be at peace! 665

Capt. Brennan (*catching up The Plough and the Stars*). Imprisonment for th' Independence of Ireland!

Lieut. Langon (*catching up the Tri-colour*). Wounds for th' Independence of Ireland!

Clitheroe. Death for th' Independence of Ireland! 670

The Three (*together*). So help us God!
> [*They drink. A bugle blows the Assembly. They hurry out. A pause.* Fluther *and* Rosie *come out of the snug;* Rosie *is linking* Fluther, *who is a little drunk. Both are in a merry mood.*

Rosie. Come on home, ower o' that, man. Are you afraid or what? Are you goin' to come home, or are you not?

(665) They think . . . be at peace!:
The famous concluding lines of Pearse's speech at the grave of O'Donovan Rossa.
(666–670) predicative statements for each of these individuals.

Fluther. Of course I'm goin' home. What ud ail me that I 678 wouldn't go?

Rosie (*lovingly*). Come on, then, oul' sport.

Officer's Voice (*giving command outside*). Irish Volunteers, by th' right, quick march!

Rosie (*putting her arm round* Fluther *and singing*):

I once had a lover, a tailor, but he could do nothin' for
me,
An' then I fell in with a sailor as strong an' as wild as th'
sea.
We cuddled an' kissed with devotion, till th' night from
th' mornin' had fled;
An' there, to our joy, a bright bouncin' boy
Was dancin' a jig in th' bed!

Dancin' a jig in th' bed, an' bawlin' for butther an'
bread.
An' there, to our joy, a bright bouncin' boy
Was dancin' a jig in th' bed!
[*They go out with their arms round each other.*

Clitheroe's Voice (*in command outside*). Dublin Battalion
of the Irish Citizen Army, by th' right, quick march!

CURTAIN
END ACT II

(678) *ud ail me: what would be
wrong with me.*

COMMENTARY ON ACT III

SUMMARY

The action of the play now moves out into the streets. It is Easter 1916, and the rising is at its height. Fluther returns with Nora—it seems she has spent the night frantically searching for Clitheroe. It is clear that the strain of separation has been too much for her, the combination of hysteria and weariness already showing signs of mental unbalance. For the others, however, the rising is the next best thing to Christmas. They take to the streets and raid the shops and public houses that have been damaged.

Clitheroe and Brennan enter carrying Langon, who has been mortally wounded. Nora rushes on and begs Clitheroe to desert his friends and come back with her. Clitheroe, torn between his wife and his comrades, hesitates for a moment before leaving, again carrying the wounded Langon. Bessie, who has been shouting insults and singing British patriotic songs like *Rule, Britannia* from her window, enters, and carries Nora back into the house. Fluther stumbles drunkenly on singing and shouting as Nora cries out, and we learn that she has gone into labour. Bessie heads off into the streets and the sound of rifle shots and machine-gun fire to fetch a doctor for Nora and the ailing Mollser.

STRUCTURE

Act III is the climax of the play: it is the accumulation of all that has gone before. Act III begins as Act I did, with Mrs. Gogan setting the scene by telling us about Nora and Fluther. But once Peter and The Covey enter, the pace of the act begins to increase. Compared with the other acts in the play, Act III is by far the most action-packed. Characters dash on and off carrying assorted stolen goods; guns explode while Nora screams hysterically; and Bessie shouts and slanders the rebels. A soldier is carried on, his stomach torn open; Bessie and Mrs. Gogan argue yet again; and Fluther manages yet again to get solidly drunk as the city falls down around him. The horror and the absurdity of war are brought together, as idealism and reality were in the previous act.

CHARACTERS

Nora, Bessie and Fluther are of particular interest in this act, Nora because of her desperate need to wrench Clitheroe from the battle, and her reactions when she fails to do so. This is indeed the determined strong-willed woman of Act I, but driven to such extreme desperation that collapse is inevitable. She does, however, raise a number of important questions. Should a woman, for instance, be so willing to allow her husband or son to be sacrificed? Should Clitheroe have deserted his comrades, who likewise desperately need his help? And what of the 'fear' (line 642) in Brennan's face, of which she speaks: surely fear is to be expected.

Bessie quietly slips a mug of milk to Mollser, and runs to help Nora after Clitheroe has left her. It is Bessie who runs for a doctor at the end of the act. But she is in no way sentimentalised as a character: throughout this act she is still the tough, loud-mouthed woman of the previous acts. It is as if she is able to channel this same strength in different directions.

Fluther braves the bullets and bombs in order to rescue Nora from the barricades, and in so doing reveals something of his character that we may not have previously suspected. The clown is also capable of being a hero.

ACT III

The corner house in a street of tenements: it is the home of the Clitheroes. The house is a long, gaunt, five-story tenement; its brick front is chipped and scarred with age and neglect. The wide and heavy hall door, flanked by two pillars, has a look of having been charred by a fire in the distant past. The door lurches a little to one side, disjointed by the continual and reckless banging when it is being closed by most of the residents. The diamond-paned fanlight is destitute of a single pane, the frame-work alone remaining. The windows, except the two looking into the front parlour (Clitheroe's room), are grimy, and are draped with fluttering and soiled fragments of lace curtains. The front parlour windows are hung with rich, comparatively, casement cloth. Five stone steps lead from the door to the path on the street. Branching on each side are railings to prevent people from falling into the area. At the left corner of the house runs a narrow lane, bisecting the street, and connecting it with another of the same kind. At the corner of the lane is a street lamp.

As the house is revealed, Mrs. Gogan *is seen helping* Mollser *to a chair, which stands on the path beside the railings, at the left side of the steps. She then wraps a shawl around* Mollser's *shoulders. It is some months later.*

Mrs. Gogan (*arranging shawl around* Mollser). Th' sun'll do you all th' good in th' world. A few more weeks o' this weather, an' there's no knowin' how well you'll be. . . . Are you comfy, now?

Mollser (*weakly and wearily*). Yis, ma; I'm all right.

Mrs. Gogan. How are you feelin'?

Mollser. Betther, ma, betther. If th' horrible sinkin' feelin' ud go, I'd be all right.

Mrs. Gogan. Ah, I wouldn't put much pass on that. Your stomach maybe's out of ordher. . . . Is th' poor breathin' any betther, d'ye think?

---

(2) *the home of the Clitheroes: Although we are told it is the Clitheroes' home, we know it is also the building in which Mrs. Gogan and Bessie live. Also, as in Act I, the dilapidated state of the building is stressed.*

(25) *Some months later: It is, in fact, Easter Week 1916.*

(34) *put much pass: place too much importance.*

(35) *breathin': A sure sign of consumption was difficulty in breathing.*

Mrs. Gogan to Mollser (seated)
'. . . With th' help o' God, you'll
be on th' mend from this out . . .'
(Act III, lines 38-9)

Nora
'They told me I shamed my husband an' th' women of Ireland be carryin' on as I was . . .'
(Act III, lines 151-3)

Mollser. Yis, yis, ma; a lot betther.

Mrs. Gogan. Well, that's somethin' anyhow. . . . With th' help o' God, you'll be on th' mend from this out. . . . D'your legs feel any sthronger undher you, d'ye think?

Mollser (*irritably*). I can't tell, ma. I think so. . . . A little.

Mrs. Gogan. Well, a little aself is somethin'. . . . I thought 42 I heard you coughin' a little more than usual last night. . . . D'ye think you were?

Mollser. I wasn't ma, I wasn't.

Mrs. Gogan. I thought I heard you, for I was kep' awake all night with th' shootin'. An' thinkin' o' that madman, Fluther, runnin' about through th' night lookin' for Nora Clitheroe to bring her back when he heard she'd gone to folly her husband, an' in dhread any minute he might come staggerin' in covered with bandages, splashed all over with th' red of his own blood, an' givin' us barely time to bring th' priest to hear th' last whisper of his final confession, as his soul was passin' through th' dark doorway o' death into th' way o' th' wondherin' dead. . . . You don't feel cold, do you?

Mollser. No, ma; I'm all right.

Mrs. Gogan. Keep your chest well covered, for that's th' delicate spot in yo . . . if there's any danger, I'll whip 60 you in again. . . . (*Looking up the street*) Oh, here's Th' 61 Covey an' oul' Pether hurryin' along. God Almighty, sthrange things is happenin' when them two is pullin' together. 64

    [The Covey *and* Peter *come in, breathless and excited.*

Mrs. Gogan (*to the two men*). Were yous far up th' town? Did yous see any sign o' Fluther or Nora? How is things lookin'? I hear they're blazin' away out o' th' G.P.O. 69 That th' Tommies is sthretched in heaps around

(42) *a little aself [itself] is somethin': a small improvement is something.*

(60) *any danger: that is, danger from gunfire.*

(61) *whip you in: take you inside quickly.*

(64) *is pullin' together: are together.*

(69) *blazin' away: shelling the building.*

(69) *G.P.O.: the General Post Office, the final stronghold of the rebels during the rising.*

Nelson's Pillar an' th' Parnell Statue, an' that th' pavin' ⁷¹ sets in O'Connell Street is nearly covered be pools o' ⁷² blood.

Peter. We seen no sign o' Nora or Fluther anywhere.

Mrs. Gogan. We should ha' held her back be main force ⁷⁵ from goin' to look for her husband. . . . God knows what's happened to her—I'm always seein' her sthretched on her back in some hospital, moanin' with th' pain of a bullet in her vitals, an' nuns thryin' to get ⁷⁹ her to take a last look at th' crucifix!

The Covey. We can do nothin'. You can't stick your nose into O'Connell Street, an' Tyler's is on fire. ⁸²

Peter. An' we seen th' Lancers— ⁸³

The Covey (*interrupting*). Throttin' along, heads in th' air; spurs an' sabres jinglin', an' lances quiverin', an' lookin' as if they were assin' themselves, "Where's these blighters, till we get a prod at them?" when there was a ⁸⁷ volley from th' Post Office that stretched half o' them, ⁸⁸ an' sent th' rest gallopin' away wondherin' how far they'd have to go before they'd feel safe.

Peter (*rubbing his hands*). "Damn it," says I to meself, "this looks like business!"

The Covey. An' then out comes General Pearse an' his ⁹³ staff, an', standin' in th' middle o' th' street, he reads th' Proclamation.

Mrs. Gogan. What proclamation?

Peter. Declarin' an Irish Republic.

Mrs. Gogan. Go to God!

Peter. The gunboat *Helga's* shellin' Liberty Hall, an' I ⁹⁹ hear the people livin' on th' quays had to crawl on their bellies to Mass with th' bullets that were flyin' around

(71) *Nelson's Pillar: a commemorative structure to Nelson, the famous British admiral; it was situated in the centre of O'Connell Street until 1966 when it was blown up, probably by the IRA.*

(71) *Parnell Statue: situated at the top of O'Connell Street, near the Rotunda Hospital.*

(72) *pavin' sets: granite paving stones.*

(75) *be main force: by physical force.*

(79) *in her vitals: in her stomach.*

(82) *Tyler's: a shoe store in O'Connell Street.*

(83) *Lancers: British soldiers of a cavalry regiment armed with lances.*

(87) *Where's these blighters . . . : spoken in imitation of a sophisticated English accent.*

(88) *a volley . . . that stretched half o' them: a round of gunfire from the GPO killed half of them.*

(93) *General Pearse: one of the principal leaders of the rising, and the orator from Act I; Pearse was both the head of the provisional government declared in the proclamation and commandant-general of its forces.*

(99) *Helga: this gunboat was brought up the Liffey to shell Liberty Hall.*

(99) *Liberty Hall: the headquarters of the Irish Transport and General Workers' Union and of the Citizen Army.*

from Boland's Mills.   102

Mrs. Gogan. God bless us, what's goin' to be th' end of it all!

Bessie (*looking out of the top window*). Maybe yous are satisfied now; maybe yous are satisfied now. Go on an' get guns if yous are men—Johnny get your gun, get your gun, get your gun! Yous are all nicely shanghaied   108 now; th' boyo hasn't a sword on his thigh now! Oh, yous are all nicely shanghaied now!

Mrs. Gogan (*warningly to* Peter *and* The Covey). S-s-sh, don't answer her. She's th' right oul' Orange bitch!   112 She's been chantin' "Rule, Britannia" all th' mornin'.   113

Peter. I hope Fluther hasn't met with any accident, he's such a wild card.   115

Mrs. Gogan. God grant it; but last night I dreamt I seen gettin' carried into th' house a sthretcher with a figure lyin' on it, stiff an' still, dhressed in th' habit of Saint Francis. An, then, I heard th' murmurs of a crowd no   119 one could see sayin' th' litany for th' dead; an' then it got   120 so dark that nothin' was seen but th' white face of th' corpse, gleamin' like a white wather-lily floatin' on th' top of a dark lake. Then a tiny whisper thrickled into me ear, sayin', "Isn't the face very like th' face o' Fluther?" an' then, with a thremblin' flutther, th' dead lips opened, an', although I couldn't hear, I knew they were sayin', "Poor oul' Fluther, afther havin' handed in his gun at last, his shakin' soul moored in th' place where th' wicked are at rest an' th' weary cease from throublin'."

Peter (*who has put on a pair of spectacles, and has been looking down the street*). Here they are, be God, here they are; just afther turnin' th' corner—Nora an' Fluther!

The Covey. She must be wounded or something—he seems to be carryin' her.

(102) *Boland's Mill: no longer in existence, this mill was a prominent feature of Dublin's quays for many years.*

(108) *shanghaied: To 'shanghai' is to render a man unconscious before shipping him as a sailor, once a common practice in the Chinese city of that name; here it means they are in trouble now.*

(112) *Orange bitch: from the Orange Order, founded in 1795 to oppose Catholic emancipation.*

(113) *'Rule, Britannia': one of the national songs of Great Britain, written by James Thomson and Thomas Arne.*

(115) *a wild card: an impetuous person.*

(119) *th' habit of Saint Francis: a special shroud worn by members of the lay Third Order of Saint Francis.*

(120) *litany for the dead: prayers for the dead.*

[Fluther *and* Nora *enter.* Fluther *has his arm around her and is half leading, half carrying her in. Her eyes are dim and hollow, her face pale and strained-looking; her hair is tossed, and her clothes are dusty.*

Mrs. Gogan (*running over to them*). God bless us, is it wounded y'are, Mrs. Clitheroe, or what?

Fluther. Ah, she's all right, Mrs. Gogan; only worn out from thravellin' an' want o' sleep. A night's rest, now, an' she'll be as fit as a fiddle. Bring her in, an' make her lie down.

Mrs. Gogan (*to* Nora). Did you hear e'er a whisper o' Mr. Clitheroe? 148

Nora (*wearily*). I could find him nowhere, Mrs. Gogan. None o' them would tell me where he was. They told me I shamed my husband an' th' women of Ireland be carryin' on as I was. . . . They said th' women must learn to be brave an' cease to be cowardly. . . . Me who risked more for love than they would risk for hate. . . . (*Raising her voice in hysterical protest*) My Jack will be killed, my Jack will be killed! . . . He is to be butchered as a sacrifice to th' dead! 158

Bessie (*from upper window*). Yous are all nicely shanghaied now! Sorra mend th' lasses that have been 160 kissin' an' cuddlin' their boys into th' sheddin' of blood! . . . Fillin' their minds with fairy tales that had no beginnin', but, please God, 'll have a bloody quick endin'! . . . Turnin' bitther into sweet, an' sweet into bitther. . . . Stabbin' in th' back th' men that are dyin' in th' threnches for them! It's a bad thing for any one that thries to jilt th' Ten Commandments, for judgements 167 are prepared for scorners an' sthripes for th' back o' fools! (*Going away from window as she sings:*)

Rule, Britannia, Britannia rules th' waves,
Britons never, never, never shall be slaves!

(148) *e'er a whisper:* have you heard anything about Clitheroe?

(158) *a sacrifice to the dead:* The Proclamation of the Irish Republic began with an appeal to Irishmen and women to support the struggle for independence of the country 'in the name of God and of the dead generations from which she receives her old tradition of nationhood.'

(160) *sorra mend:* little pity for.

(167) *jilt th' Ten Commandments . . . :* Those who ignore the Ten Commandments will suffer in Hell, while those who don't know better will be whipped, or punished in some such way.

Fluther (*with a roar up at the window*). Y'ignorant oul' throllope, you!

Mrs. Gogan (*to* Nora). He'll come home safe enough to you, you'll find, Mrs. Clitheroe; afther all, there's a power o' women that's handed over sons an' husbands 176 to take a runnin' risk in th' fight they're wagin'.

Nora. I can't help thinkin' every shot fired'll be fired at Jack, an' every shot fired at Jack 'll be fired at me. What do I care for th' others? I can think only of me own self. . . . An' there's no woman gives a son or a husband to be killed—if they say it, they're lyin', lyin', against God, Nature, an' against themselves! . . . One blasted hussy at 183 a barricade told me to go home an' not be thryin' to dishearten th' men . . . That I wasn't worthy to bear a son to a man that was out fightin' for freedom. . . . I clawed at her, an' smashed her in th' face till we were separated. . . . I was pushed down th' street, an' I cursed them—cursed the rebel ruffians an' Volunteers that had dhragged me ravin' mad into th' sthreets to seek me 190 husband!

Peter. You'll have to have patience, Nora. We all have to put up with twarthers an' tormentors in this world.

The Covey. If they were fightin' for anything worth while, I wouldn' mind.

Fluther (*to* Nora). Nothin' derogatory 'll happen to Mr. Clitheroe. You'll find, now, in th' finish up it'll be vice versa.

Nora. Oh, I know that wherever he is, he's thinkin' of wantin' to be with me. I know he's longin' to be passin' his hand through me hair, to be caressin' me neck, to fondle me hand an' to feel me kisses clingin' to his mouth. . . . An' he stands wherever he is because he's brave? (*Vehemently*) No, but because he's a coward, a 204 coward, a coward!

Mrs. Gogan. Oh, they're not cowards anyway.

(176) *a power o' women: a lot of women.*
(183) *hussy: a worthless woman.*
(190) *Volunteers that had dhragged me: not meant literally: Nora blames the Volunteers for bringing about the circumstances that caused her to risk her life searching for Clitheroe.*
(204) *An' he stands . . . brave?: If Clitheroe wants all these things he should be brave enough to admit it.*

Nora (*with denunciatory anger*). I tell you they're afraid to say they're afraid! . . . Oh, I saw it, I saw it, Mrs. Gogan. . . . At th' barricade in North King Street I saw fear glowin' in all their eyes. . . . An' in th' middle o' th' sthreet was somethin' huddled up in a horrible tangled heap. . . . His face was jammed again th' stones, an' his arm was twisted round his back. . . . An' every twist of his body was a cry against th' terrible thing that had happened to him. . . . An' I saw they were afraid to look at it. . . . An' some o' them laughed at me, but th' laugh was a frightened one. . . . An' some o' them shouted at me, but th' shout had in it th' shiver o' fear. . . . I tell you they were afraid, afraid, afraid!

Mrs. Gogan (*leading her towards the house*). Come on in, dear. If you'd been a little longer together, th' wrench asundher wouldn't have been so sharp.   221
222

Nora. Th' agony I'm in since he left me has thrust away every rough thing he done, an' every unkind word he spoke; only th' blossoms that grew out of our lives are before me now; shakin' their colours before me face, an' breathin' their sweet scent on every thought springin' up in me mind, till, sometimes, Mrs. Gogan, sometimes I think I'm goin' mad!   223
229

Mrs. Gogan. You'll be a lot betther when you have a little lie down.

Nora (*turning towards* Fluther *as she is going in*). I don't know what I'd have done, only for Fluther. I'd have been lyin' in th' streets, only for him. . . . (*As she goes in*) They have dhriven away th' little happiness life had to spare for me. He has gone from me for ever, for ever. . . . Oh, Jack, Jack, Jack! ↱
[*She is led in by* Mrs. Gogan *as* Bessie *comes out with a shawl around her shoulders. She passes by them with her head in the air. When they have gone in, she gives a mug of milk to* Mollser *silently.*]

Fluther. Which of yous has th' tossers?   243

(221) been a little longer together: been married longer.
(222) so sharp: so painful.
(223–229) See Introduction (page 16).
(243) tossers: two pieces of wood used for tossing coins. They are about to play a game of pitch-and-toss.

The Covey. I have.

Bessie (*as she is passing them to go down the street*). You an' your Leadhers an' their sham-battle soldiers has landed a body in a nice way, havin' to go an' ferret out a bit o' bread God knows where. . . . Why aren't yous in th' G.P.O. if yous are men? It's paler an' paler yous are gettin'. . . . A lot o' vipers, that's what th' Irish people is! [*She goes out.*

Fluther. Never mind her. . . . (*To* The Covey) Make a start an' keep us from th' sin o' idleness. (*To* Mollser) Well, how are you to-day, Mollser, oul' son? What are you dhrinkin', milk?

Mollser. Grand, Fluther, grand, thanks. Yis, milk.

Fluther. You couldn't get a betther thing down you. . . . This turn-up has done one good thing, anyhow; you can't get dhrink anywhere, an' if it lasts a week, I'll be so used to it that I won't think of a pint.

The Covey (*who has taken from his pocket two worn coins and a thin strip of wood about four inches long*). What's th' bettin'?

Peter. Heads, a juice.

Fluther. Harps, a tanner.
　　　　[The Covey *places the coins on the strip of wood, and flips them up into the air. As they jingle on the ground the distant boom of a big gun is heard. They stand for a moment listening.*

Fluther. What th' hell's that?

The Covey. It's like th' boom of a big gun!

Fluther. Surely to God they're not goin' to use artillery on us?

The Covey (*scornfully*). Not goin'! (*Vehemently*)

---

(246) *sham-battle soldiers: incapable soldiers.*

(247) *ferret out: search out with great difficulty.*

(249) *paler and paler: growing more cowardly by the minute.*

(250) *vipers: treacherous people.*

(258) *turn-up: turn of events.*

(264) *Heads, a juice* [deuce]: *If the coin shows heads, you win twopence.*

(265) *Harps, a tanner: If it shows the side of the coin with a harp, the person wins sixpence.*

Wouldn't they use anything on us, man?

Fluther. Aw, holy Christ, that's not playin' the game!　　276

Peter (*plaintively*). What would happen if a shell landed here now?

The Covey (*ironically*). You'd be off to heaven in a fiery chariot.　　280

Peter. In spite of all th' warnin's that's ringin' around us, are you goin' to start your pickin' at me again?

Fluther. Go on, toss them again, toss them again. . . . Harps, a tanner.

Peter. Heads, a juice.　　　　[The Covey *tosses the coins.*

Fluther (*as the coins fall*). Let them roll, let them roll. Heads, be God!
　　　[Bessie *runs in excitedly. She has a new hat on her head, a fox fur round her neck over her shawl, three umbrellas under her right arm, and a box of biscuits under her left. She speaks rapidly and breathlessly.*

Bessie. They're breakin' into th' shops, they're breakin'　293 into th' shops! Smashin' th' windows, batterin' in th' doors, an' whippin' away everything! An' th' Volunteers is firin' on them. I seen two men an' a lassie　296 pushin' a piano down th' sthreet, an' th' sweat rollin' off them thryin' to get it up on th' pavement; an' an oul' wan that must ha' been seventy lookin' as if she'd dhrop every minute with th' dint o' heart beatin', thryin' to　300 pull a big double bed out of a broken shop-window! I was goin' to wait till I dhressed meself from th' skin out.　302

Mollser (*to Bessie, as she is going in*). Help me in, Bessie; I'm feelin' curious.　　304
　　　[Bessie *leaves the looted things in the house, and, rapidly returning, helps* Mollser *in.*

(276) *playin' th' game: adhering to the 'rules' of war.*
(280) *fiery chariot: as in the Old Testament.*
(293) *They're breakin' into the shops: Some of the people of Dublin did take advantage of circumstances to loot the shops in the city centre.*
(296) *Volunteers is firin' on them: The Volunteers did in fact fire on looting civilians.*
(300) *with th' dint o': by dint of, by force of.*
(302) *dhressed meself from th' skin out: had a whole wardrobe of clothes.*
(304) *I'm feelin' curious: I'm feeling ill.*

The Covey. Th' selfishness of that one—she waited till she got all she could carry before she'd come to tell anyone!

Fluther (*running over to the door of the house and shouting in to* Bessie). Ay, Bessie, did you hear of e'er a pub gettin' a shake up? 311

Bessie (*inside*). I didn't hear o' none.

Fluther (*in a burst of enthusiasm*). Well, you're goin' to 313 hear of one soon!

The Covey. Come on, man, an' don't be wastin' time.

Peter (*to them as they are about to run off*). Ay, ay, are you goin' to leave me here?

Fluther. Are you goin' to leave yourself here?

Peter (*anxiously*). Didn't yous hear her sayin' they were firin' on them?

The Covey and Fluther (*together*). Well?

Peter. Supposin' I happened to be potted? 322

Fluther. We'd give you a Christian burial, anyhow.

The Covey (*ironically*). Dhressed up in your regimentals. 324

Peter (*to* The Covey, *passionately*). May th' all-lovin' God give you a hot knock one o' these days, me young Covey, 326 tuthorin' Fluther up now to be tiltin' at me, an' crossin' 327 me with his mockeries an' jibin'!
[*A fashionably dressed, middle-aged, stout* 329 *woman comes hurriedly in, and makes for the group. She is almost fainting with fear.*

The Woman. For Gawd's sake, will one of you kind men 332 show any safe way for me to get to Wrathmines? . . . I 333 was foolish enough to visit a friend, thinking the howl 334

311 a shake up: damaged by the fighting.
313 Well, you're goin' to: Fluther intends to loot a pub.
322 potted: hit by a bullet.
324 regimentals: Foresters' costume.
326 give you a hot knock: punish you.
327 tuthorin': teaching.
327 tiltin' at me: jeering me.
329 Often in productions of this play, directors do not include this woman. She adds very little to the play as a whole, and slows down the action of this section. As a character she is hardly believable, and her appearance so brief that nothing of worth is lost by her exclusion.
332 Gawd: 'posh' pronunciation of 'God'.
333 Wrathmines [Rathmines]: O'Casey gives her this affected accent because she comes from what was a well-to-do part of Dublin.
334 howl [whole].

thing was a joke, and now I cawn't get a car or a tram to take me home—isn't it awful?

Fluther. I'm afraid, ma'am, one way is as safe as another.

Woman. And what am I gowing to do? Oh, isn't this awful? . . . I'm so different from others. . . . The mowment I hear a shot, my legs give way under me—I cawn't stir, I'm paralysed—isn't it awful?

Fluther (*moving away*). It's a derogatory way to be, right enough, ma'am.

Woman (*catching* Fluther's *coat*). Creeping along the street there, with my head down and my eyes half shut, a bullet whizzed past within an inch of my nowse. . . . I 346 had to lean against the wall for a long time, gasping for breath—I nearly passed away—it was awful! . . . I wonder, would you kind men come some of the way and see me safe?

Fluther. I have to go away, ma'am, to thry an' save a few things from th' burnin' buildin's. 352

The Covey. Come on, then, or there won't be anything left to save.   [The Covey *and* Fluther *hurry away.*

Woman (*to* Peter). Wasn't it an awful thing for me to leave my friend's house? Wasn't it an idiotic thing to do? . . . I haven't the slightest idea where I am. . . . You have a kind face, sir. Could you possibly come and pilot me in 358 the direction of Wrathmines?

Peter (*indignantly*). D'ye think I'm goin' to risk me life throttin' in front of you? An' maybe get a bullet that 361 would gimme a game leg or something that would leave 362 me a jibe an' a jeer to Fluther an' th' young Covey for th' rest o' me days!
    [*With an indignant toss of his head he walks into the house.*

The Woman (*going out*). I know I'll fall down in a dead

(346) *nowse* [*nose*].
(352) *save a few things: a nice way of saying he intends looting.*
(358) *pilot: lead in the right direction.*
(361) *throttin'* [*trotting*].
(362) *gimme* [*give me*].
(362) *game leg: crippled leg.*

111

faint if I hear another shot go off anyway near me—isn't it awful!

[Mrs. Gogan *comes out of the house pushing a pram before her. As she enters the street* Bessie *rushes out, follows* Mrs. Gogan, *and catches hold of the pram, stopping* Mrs. Gogan's *progress.*

Bessie. Here, where are you goin' with that? How quick you were, me lady, to clap your eyes on th' pram. . . . 376 Maybe you don't know that Mrs. Sullivan, before she 377 went to spend Easther with her people in Dunboyne, gave me sthrict injunctions to give an accasional look to 379 see if it was still standin' where it was left in th' corner of th' lobby.

Mrs. Gogan. That remark of yours, Mrs. Bessie Burgess, requires a little considheration, seein' that th' pram was 383 left on our lobby, an' not on yours; a foot or two a little to th' left of th' jamb of me own room door; nor is it 385 needful to mention th' name of th' person that gave a 386 squint to see if it was there th' first thing in th' mornin', 387 an' th' last thing in th' stillness o' th' night; never failin' to realize that her eyes couldn't be goin' wrong, be sthretchin' out her arm an' runnin' her hand over th' pram, to make sure that th' sight was no deception! 391 Moreover, somethin's tellin' me that th' runnin' hurry 392 of an inthrest you're takin' in it now is a sudden ambition to use th' pram for a purpose that a loyal woman of law an' ordher would stagger away from! 395

[*She gives the pram a sudden push that pulls* Bessie *forward.*

Bessie (*still holding the pram*). There's not as much as one body in th' house that doesn't know that it wasn't Bessie 399 Burgess that was always shakin' her voice complainin' 400 about people leavin' bassinettes in th' way of them that, 401 week in an' week out, had to pay their rent, an' always had to find a regular accommodation for her own furniture in her own room. . . . An' as for law an' ordher, puttin' aside th' harp an' shamrock, Bessie

---

(376) *clap your eyes on th' pram:* see and take the pram.

(377) *Mrs. Sullivan:* the owner of the pram.

(379) *injunctions:* strict orders to look after the pram.

(383) *seein' that:* since.

(385) *a foot or two . . . me own room door:* Mrs. Gogan argues that since the pram was left near her door, she has more right to it.

(386) *th' name of th' person:* referring to herself.

(387) *gave a squint:* looked to see of it was there.

(391) *no deception:* Not content just to see it, she always touched it to make doubly sure it was there.

(392) *runnin' hurry:* the sudden interest she has in the pram.

(395) *woman of law an' ordher . . . :* If Bessie was as God-fearing as she makes herself out to be, she would have no use for the pram.

(399) *not as . . . doesn't know:* everybody knows.

(400) *shakin' her voice:* raising her voice in complaint.

(401) *bassinette [bassinet]:* a child's pram.

112

Burgess 'll have as much respect as she wants for th' lion an' unicorn! 407

Peter (*appearing at the door*). I think I'll go with th' pair of yous an' see th' fun. A fella might as well chance it, anyhow.

Mrs. Gogan (*taking no notice of* Peter, *and pushing the pram on another step*). Take your rovin' lumps o' hands from pattin' th' bassinette, if you please, ma'am; an', 413 steppin' from th' threshold of good manners, let me tell 414 you, Mrs. Burgess, that's it's a fat wondher to Jennie 415 Gogan that a lady-like singer o' hymns like yourself would lower her thoughts from sky-thinkin' to sthretch 417 out her arm in a sly-seekin' way to pinch anything 418 dhriven asthray in th' confusion of th' battle our boys is 419 makin' for th' freedom of their counthry!

Peter (*laughing and rubbing his hands together*). Hee, hee, hee, hee, hee! I'll go with th' pair o' yous an' give yous a hand.

Mrs. Gogan (*with a rapid turn of her head as she shoves the pram forward*). Get up in th' prambulator an' we'll wheel you down.

Bessie (*to* Mrs. Gogan). Poverty an' hardship has sent Bessie Burgess to abide with sthrange company, but she 428 always knew them she had to live with from backside to breakfast time; an' she can tell them, always havin' had 430 a Christian kinch on her conscience, that a passion for 431 thievin' an' pinchin' would find her soul a foreign place to live in, an' that her present intention is quite th' 433 lofty-hearted one of pickin' up anything shaken up an' 434 scatthered about in th' loose confusion of a general plundher!
    [*By this time they have disappeared from view.* Peter *is following, when the boom of a big gun in the distance brings him to a quick halt.*

Peter. God Almighty, that's th' big gun again! God forbid any harm would happen to them, but sorra mind I'd

(407) **lion an' unicorn**: *In answer to Mrs. Gogan's earlier point (see line 395 above) about Bessie's not wishing to break the law, Bessie justifies her actions by saying that it is British and not Irish law she respects.*

(413) **pattin'**: *touching.*

(414) **steppin' from th' threshold of good manners**: *placing good manners to one side for a moment.*

(415) **it's a fat wondher**: *it is amazing.*

(417) **lower her thoughts . . . .**: *that such a saintly person as Bessie would contemplate looting.*

(418) **sly-seekin'**: *devious.*

(419) **dhriven asthray** [*driven astray*]: *scattered in the confusion.*

(428) **abide with strange company**: *live with and put up with strange people.*

(430) **backside to breakfast time**: *from morning to night.*

(431) **Christian kinch**: *Christian sense of right and wrong.*

(433) **foreign place to live in**: *her soul would not allow her to steal.*

(434) **lofty-hearted one of . . . .**: *Bessie insists that she will not be looting, but gathering things lost in the confusion of the battle: a case of 'waste not want not'.*

113

mind if they met with a dhrop in their mad endeyvours 442
to plundher an' desthroy.

> [*He looks down the street for a moment, then
> runs to the hall door of the house, which is
> open, and shuts it with a vicious pull; he then
> goes to the chair in which* Mollser *had sat, sits
> down, takes out his pipe, lights it and begins to
> smoke with his head carried at a haughty angle.* 449
> The Covey *comes staggering in with a ten-
> stone sack of flour on his back. On the top of
> the sack is a ham. He goes over to the door,
> pushes it with his head, and finds he can't open
> it; he turns slightly in the direction of* Peter.]

The Covey (*to* Peter). Who shut th' door? . . . (*He kicks at
it*) Here, come on an' open it, will you? This isn't a
mot's hand-bag I've got on me back. 457

Peter. Now, me young Covey, d'ye think I'm goin' to be
your lackey? 459

The Covey (*angrily*). Will you open th' door, y'oul'—

Peter (*shouting*). Don't be assin' me to open any door, 461
don't be assin' me to open any door for you. . . . Makin'
a shame an' a sin o' th' cause that good men are fightin'
for. . . . Oh, God forgive th' people that, instead o'
burnishin' th' work th' boys is doin' to-day with quiet 465
honesty an' patience, is revilin' their sacrifices with a
riot of lootin' an' roguery!

The Covey. Isn't your own eyes leppin' out o' your head
with envy that you haven't th' guts to ketch a few o' th' 469
things that God is givin' to His chosen people? . . .
Y'oul' hypocrite, if everyone was blind you'd steal a 471
cross off an ass's back!

Peter (*very calmly*). You're not going to make me lose me
temper; you can go on with your proddin' as long as
you like; goad an' goad an' goad away; hee, hee, heee!
I'll not lose me temper.

> [*Somebody opens door and* The Covey *goes in.*]

(442) *sorra mind I'd mind: it's little
I'd mind.*

(442) *if they met with a dhrop: If a
shell landed on them it
would be their own fault.*

(449) *carried at a haughty angle:
proudly; with his head in the
air.*

(457) *a mot's hand-bag: a girl-
friend's hand-bag.*

(459) *lackey: servant.*

(461) *assin' [asking].*

(465) *burnishin': polishing; the
people should refrain from
temptation instead of making
a mockery of the rebels'
cause.*

(469) *th' guts to ketch: the nerve to
catch; The Covey correctly
points out that Peter has
adopted this moral tone
simply because he has not the
courage to loot himself.*

(471) *if everyone was blind . . . :
you would steal anything
given half a chance.*

The Covey (*inside, mockingly*). Cuckoo-oo!

Peter (*running to the door and shouting in a blaze of passion as he follows* The Covey *in*). You lean, long, lanky lath of a lowsey bastard. . . . (*Following him in*) ₄₈₁ Lowsey bastard, lowsey bastard!

> [Bessie *and* Mrs. Gogan *enter, the pride of a great joy illuminating their faces. Bessie is pushing the pram, which is filled with clothes and boots; on the top of the boots and clothes is a fancy table, which* Mrs. Gogan *is holding on with her left hand, while with her right hand she holds a chair on the top of her head. They are heard talking to each other before they enter.*

Mrs. Gogan (*outside*). I don't remember ever havin' seen such lovely pairs as them, (*they appear*) with th' pointed toes an' th' cuban heels. ₄₉₄

Bessie. They'll go grand with th' dhresses we're afther liftin', when we've stitched a sthray bit o' silk to lift th' ₄₉₆ bodices up a little bit higher, so as to shake th' shame ₄₉₇ out o' them, an' make them fit for women that hasn't ₄₉₈ lost themselves in th' nakedness o' th' times. ₄₉₉

> [*They fussily carry in the chair, the table, and some of the other goods. They return to bring in the rest.*

Peter (*at door, sourly to* Mrs. Gogan). Ay, you. Mollser looks as if she was goin' to faint, an' your youngster is roarin' in convulsions in her lap.

Mrs. Gogan (*snappily*). She's never any other way but faintin'!

> [*She goes to go in with some things in her arms, when a shot from a rifle rings out. She and* Bessie *make a bolt for the door, which* Peter, *in a panic, tries to shut before they have got inside.*

Mrs. Gogan. Ay, ay, ay, you cowardly oul' fool, what are you thryin' to shut th' door on us for?

---

(481) *lath: a thin strip of wood.*
(494) *cuban heels: moderately high heels.*
(496) *liftin': stealing; a slip of the tongue on Bessie' part.*
(496) *when we've stitched . . . : Ironically, Bessie adopts a moral tone in discussing how the dresses can be made more respectable when in fact the dresses have been stolen.*
(497) *lift th' bodices up a little higher: raise the low necklines.*
(498) *shake th' shame out o' them: make them more respectable.*
(499) *th' nakedness o' th' times: another reference to low necklines.*

[*They retreat tumultuously inside. A pause; then* Captain Brennan *comes in supporting* Lieutenant Langon, *whose arm is around* Brennan's *neck.* Langon's *face, which is ghastly white, is momentarily convulsed with spasms of agony. He is in a state of collapse, and* Brennan *is almost carrying him. After a few moments,* Clitheroe, *pale, and in a state of calm nervousness, follows, looking back in the direction from which he came, a rifle, held at the ready, in his hands.*

Capt. Brennan (*savagely to* Clitheroe). Why did you fire over their heads? Why didn't you fire to kill? 526

Clitheroe. No, no, Bill; bad as they are they're Irish men an' women. 528

Capt. Brennan (*savagely*). Irish be damned! Attackin' an' mobbin' th' men that are riskin' their lives for them. If these slum lice gather at our heels again, plug one o' them, or I'll soon shock them with a shot or two meself! 531

Lieut. Langon (*moaningly*). My God, is there ne'er an ambulance knockin' around anywhere? ... Th' stomach is ripped out o' me; I feel it—o-o-oh Christ!

Capt. Brennan. Keep th' heart up, Jim; we'll soon get help, now.
[Nora *rushes wildly out of the house and flings her arms round the neck of* Clitheroe *with a fierce and joyous insistence. Her hair is down, her face is haggard, but her eyes are agleam with the light of happy relief.*

Nora. Jack, Jack, Jack; God be thanked . . . be thanked. . . . He has been kind and merciful to His poor hand-maiden. . . . My Jack, my own Jack, that I thought was lost is found, that I thought was dead is alive again! . . . 546
Oh, God be praised for ever, evermore! . . . My poor Jack. . . . Kiss me, kiss me, Jack, kiss your own Nora!

(526) *Why did you fire over their heads?: referring to the looters. (See the Introduction, page 12).*

(528) *they're Irish men an' women: Clitheroe recognises the absurdity of shooting at his own people.*

(531) *slum lice: contemptible people.*

(531) *plug one: shoot one.*

(546) *that I thought was lost . . . : Notice the biblical phraseology here: Nora is quoting almost exactly from the story of the prodigal son and the words of his father on his return.*

Bessie
  'They'll go grand with th' dhresses we're afther liftin' . . .' (Act III, lines 495-6)

Langon
  'I'm dyin', I think, I'm dyin'!'
  (Act III, lines 658-9)

Clitheroe (*kissing her, and speaking brokenly*). My Nora; my little, beautiful Nora, I wish to God I'd never left you.

Nora. It doesn't matter—not now, not now, Jack. It will make us dearer than ever to each other. . . . Kiss me, kiss me again.

Clitheroe. Now, for God's sake, Nora, don't make a scene. 555

Nora. I won't, I won't; I promise, I promise, Jack; honest to God. I'll be silent an' brave to bear th' joy of feelin' you safe in my arms again. . . . It's hard to force away th' tears of happiness at th' end of an awful agony.

Bessie (*from the upper window*). Th' Minsthrel Boys 560 aren't feelin' very comfortable now. Th' big guns has knocked all th' harps out of their hands. General 562 Clitheroe 'd rather be unlacin' his wife's bodice than standin' at a barricade. . . . An' th' professor of chicken-butcherin' there, finds he's up against somethin' a little 565 tougher even than his own chickens, an' that's sayin' a lot!

Capt. Brennan (*up to* Bessie). Shut up, y'oul' hag!

Bessie (*down to* Brennan). Choke th' chicken, choke th' chicken, choke th' chicken!

Lieut. Langon. For God's sake, Bill, bring me some place where me wound 'll be looked afther. . . . Am I to die before anything is done to save me?

Capt. Brennan (*to* Clitheroe). Come on, Jack. We've got to get help for Jim, here—have you no thought for his pain an' danger?

Bessie. Choke th' chicken, choke th' chicken, choke th' chicken!

Clitheroe (*to* Nora). Loosen me, darling, let me go.

(555) *don't make a scene: Clitheroe is clearly concerned about what people watching might think.*

(560) *Th' Minsthrel Boys: another reference to ancient Ireland, taken from a ballad of the same name by Thomas Moore.*

(562) *harps: The same ballad makes a reference to the harps that the minstrels supposedly carried with them into battle.*

(565) *professor of chicken-butcherin': Bessie is talking to Brennan who works as a chicken butcher.*

Nora (*clinging to him*). No, no, no, I'll not let you go! Come on, come up to our home, Jack, my sweetheart, my lover, my husband, an' we'll forget th' last few terrible days! . . . I look tired now, but a few hours of happy rest in your arms will bring back th' bloom of freshness again, an' you will be glad, you will be glad, glad . . . glad!

Lieut. Langon. Oh, if I'd kep' down only a little longer, I mightn't ha' been hit! Everyone else escapin', an' me gettin' me belly ripped asundher! . . . I couldn't scream, couldn't even scream. . . . D'ye think I'm really badly wounded, Bill? Me clothes seem to be all soakin' wet. . . . It's blood . . . My God, it must be me own blood!

Capt. Brennan (*to* Clitheroe). Go on, Jack, bid her good-bye with another kiss, an' be done with it! D'ye want Langon to die in me arms while you're dallyin' with 595 your Nora?

Clitheroe (*to* Nora). I must go, I must go, Nora. I'm sorry we met at all. . . . It couldn't be helped—all other ways were blocked be th' British. . . . Let me go, can't you, Nora? D'ye want me to be unthrue to me comrades? 600

Nora. No, I won't let you go. . . . I want you to be thrue to me, Jack. . . . I'm your dearest comrade; I'm your thruest comrade. . . . They only want th' comfort of havin' you in th' same danger as themselves. . . . Oh, Jack, I can't let you go!

Clitheroe. You must, Nora, you must.

Nora. All last night at th' barricades I sought you, Jack. . . . I didn't think of th' danger—I could only think of you. . . . I asked for you everywhere. . . . Some o' them laughed. . . . I was pushed away, but I shoved back. . . . Some o' them even sthruck me . . . an' I screamed an' screamed your name!

Clitheroe (*in fear her action would give him future shame*). What possessed you to make a show of yourself, 614

---

(595) *dallyin': wasting time.*
(600) *unthrue: to let my comrades down in their hour of need.*
(614) *a show of yourself: still concerned about his reputation, Clitheroe shows little gratitude or understanding for Nora and what she did for him.*

like that? . . . What way d'ye think I'll feel when I'm told my wife was bawlin' for me at th' barricades? What are you more than any other woman?

Nora. No more, maybe; but you are more to me than any other man, Jack. . . . I didn't mean any harm, honestly, Jack. . . . I couldn't help it. . . . I shouldn't have told you. . . . My love for you made me mad with terror.

Clitheroe (*angrily*). They'll say now that I sent you out th' way I'd have an excuse to bring you home. . . . Are you goin' to turn all th' risks I'm takin' into a laugh?

Lieut. Langon. Let me lie down, let me lie down, Bill; th' pain would be easier, maybe, lyin' down. . . . Oh, God, have mercy on me!

Capt. Brennan (*to* Langon). A few steps more, Jim, a few steps more; thry to stick it for a few steps more.

Lieut. Langon. Oh, I can't, I can't, I can't!

Capt. Brennan (*to* Clitheroe). Are you comin', man, or are you goin' to make an arrangement for another honeymoon? . . . If you want to act th' renegade, say so, an' we'll be off!

Bessie (*from above*). Runnin' from th' Tommies—choke th' chicken. Runnin' from th' Tommies—choke th' chicken!

Clitheroe (*savagely to* Brennan). Damn you, man, who wants to act th' renegade? (*To* Nora) Here, let go your hold; let go I say!

Nora (*clinging to* Clitheroe, *and indicating* Brennan). Look, Jack, look at th' anger in his face; look at th' fear glintin' in his eyes. . . . He himself's afraid, afraid, afraid . . . He wants you to go th' way he'll have th' chance of death sthrikin' you an' missin' him! . . . Turn round an' look at him, Jack, look at him, look at him! . . . His very soul is cold . . . shiverin' with th' thought

(616) bawlin': crying like a baby.
(623) th' way: so that.
(633) renegade: deserter.

120

of what may happen to him. . . . It is his fear that is thryin' to frighten you from recognizin' th' same fear that is in your own heart!

Clitheroe (*struggling to release himself from* Nora). Damn you, woman, will you let me go!

Capt. Brennan (*fiercely, to* Clitheroe). Why are you beggin' her to let you go? Are you afraid of her, or what? Break her hold on you, man, or go up, an' sit on her lap! 655
    [Clitheroe *trying roughly to break her hold.*

Nora (*imploringly*). Oh, Jack. . . . Jack. . . . Jack!

Lieut. Langon (*agonisingly*). Brennan, a priest; I'm dyin', I think, I'm dyin'!

Clitheroe (*to* Nora). If you won't do it quietly, I'll have to make you! (*To* Brennan) Here, hold this gun, you, for a minute.   [*He hands the gun to* Brennan.

Nora (*pitifully*). Please, Jack. . . . You're hurting me, Jack. . . . Honestly. . . . Oh, you're hurting . . . me! . . . I won't, I won't, I won't! . . . Oh, Jack, I gave you everything you asked of me. . . . Don't fling me from you, now!
    [*He roughly loosens her grip, and pushes her away from him.* Nora *sinks to the ground and lies there.*

Nora (*weakly*). Ah, Jack. . . . Jack. . . . Jack!

Clitheroe (*taking the gun back from* Brennan). Come on, come on.
    [*They go out.* Bessie *looks at* Nora *lying on the street, for a few moments, then, leaving the window, she comes out, runs over to* Nora, *lifts her up in her arms, and carries her swiftly into the house. A short pause, then down the street is heard a wild, drunken yell; it comes nearer, and* Fluther *enters, frenzied, wild-eyed, mad, roaring drunk. In his arms is an earthen half-*

(655) *sit on her lap: as a child would sit on its mother's lap.*

121

gallon jar of whisky; streaming from one of the 682
*pockets of his coat is the arm of a new tunic
shirt; on his head is a woman's vivid blue hat
with gold lacing, all of which he has looted.*

Fluther (*singing in a frenzy*):
Fluther's a jolly good fella! . . . Fluther's a jolly good
fella!
Up th' rebels! . . . That nobody can deny!
[*He beats on the door.*
Get us a mug or a jug, or somethin', some o' yous, one o' 691
yous, will yous, before I lay one o' yous out! . . .
(*Looking down the street*) Bang an' fire away for all
Fluther cares. . . . (*Banging at door*) Come down an'
open th' door, some of yous, one o' yous, will yous,
before I lay some o' yous out! . . . Th' whole city can
topple home to hell, for Fluther!
[*Inside the house is heard a scream from* Nora,
followed by a moan.

Fluther (*singing furiously*):
That nobody can deny, that nobody can deny,
For Fluther's a jolly good fella, Fluther's a jolly good
fella,
Fluther's a jolly good fella . . . Up th' rebels! That
nobody can deny!
[*His frantic movements cause him to spill some of
the whiskey out of the jar.*
Blast you, Fluther, don't be spillin' th' precious liquor!
(*He kicks at the door*). Ay, give us a mug or a jug, or
somethin', one o' yous, some o' yous, will yous, before I
lay one o' yous out!
[*The door suddenly opens, and* Bessie, *coming
out, grips him by the collar.* 713

Bessie (*indignantly*). You bowsey, come in ower o' that.
. . . I'll thrim your thricks o' dhrunken dancin' for you, 715
an' none of us knowin' how soon we'll bump into a
world we were never in before! 717

Fluther (*as she is pulling him in*). Ay, th' jar, th' jar, th'
jar!

(682) *earthen half-gallon jar of
whisky: old-fashioned
earthenware container with a
single handle.*
(691) *a mug or a jug: Fluther is
desperate for something to
drink his whisky from.*
(713) *grips him: It is Bessie's turn
to quieten Fluther, but for
Nora's sake, not her own.*
(715) *thrim your thricks: put a stop
to your cavorting.*
(717) *a world we were never in: the
after-life.*

[*A short pause, then again is heard a scream of pain from* Nora. *The door opens and* Mrs. Gogan *and* Bessie *are seen standing at it.*

Bessie. Fluther would go, only he's too dhrunk. . . . Oh, God, isn't it a pity he's so dhrunk! We'll have to thry to get a docthor somehwere.

Mrs. Gogan. I'd be afraid to go. . . . Besides, Mollser's ₇₂₆ terrible bad. I don't think you'll get a docthor to come. It's hardly any use goin'.

Bessie (*determinedly*). I'll risk it. . . . Give her a little of Fluther's whisky. . . . It's th' fright that's brought it on ₇₃₀ her so soon. . . . Go on back to her, you.

[Mrs. Gogan *goes in, and* Bessie *softly closes the door. She is moving forward, when the sound of some rifle shots, and the tok, tok, tok of a distant machine-gun bring her to a sudden halt. She hesitates for a moment, then she tightens her shawl round her, as if it were a shield, then she firmly and swiftly goes out.*

Bessie (*as she goes out*). Oh, God, be Thou my help in time o' throuble. An' shelter me safely in th' shadow of Thy wings!

CURTAIN

END ACT III

(726) *I'd be afraid: Though they have already been out looting in the streets, it is likely that with each passing moment things are becoming more dangerous.*

(730) *th' fright that's brought it on: Nora has prematurely gone into labour.*

COMMENTARY ON ACT IV

SUMMARY

It is important to bear in mind that throughout this act the setting, which is Bessie's squalid attic room, is in semi-darkness, with the two candles, the fire, and the red glare from the burning buildings as the only sources of light. The mood and atmosphere, in contrast to the previous three acts, is oppressive. Nora has lost the child, and Mollser has finally succumbed to consumption, and the child and Mollser lie in the same coffin. Nora has gone insane and may never recover. Brennan returns in his civilian clothes with the news of Clitheroe's death. We meet some English soldiers who are on the look-out for a sniper. The coffin is taken away and Peter, The Covey, Fluther and Brennan are imprisoned for the night in a church. Bessie, while pushing Nora from the window, is shot twice in the back by the English soldiers who mistake her for the sniper. Fully aware that she is about to die, Bessie asks Nora for her hand. This is the only thing Bessie has asked of anybody, but her final plea goes unanswered. As the play draws to an end, so too does the rising, as the Volunteers in the GPO are overpowered.

STRUCTURE AND CHARACTERS

Although no fewer than four of the play's characters are dead by the close of this act and another has gone insane, there is still enough power and energy to prevent it sinking beneath a wave of gloom and despair. Why is this? Probably because the final message of the play is that life goes on regardless. The wheel comes full circle, and things continue as if nothing ever happened. Fluther and The Covey, undaunted, prod and jeer Peter even as they carry the coffin from the house. Peter, reacting, returns to the same complicated, argumentative language of Acts I and II. Mrs. Gogan concentrates on her favourite subject: death. Admittedly the casualties are great, but by the end of Act IV they have become the scars of one more battle. Even The Covey has not given up his faith in socialist emancipation.

The events recorded in the play may be despairing, but the people are not. Bessie, whom we may have misjudged earlier on in the play, is undoubtedly a heroic figure. The others are survivors, with the right combination of weaknesses and strengths—even Nora, whose retreat into insanity is in itself a survival tactic. When all else collapses, they remain upright, they remain firm.

ACT IV

The living-room of Bessie Burgess. *It is one of two small attic rooms (the other, used as a bedroom, is to the Left), the ceiling slopes up towards the back, giving to the apartment a look of compressed confinement. In the centre of the ceiling is a small skylight. There is an unmistakable air of poverty bordering on destitution.* 6 *The paper on the walls is torn and soiled, particularly near the fire where the cooking is done, and near the washstand where the washing is done. The fireplace is to the Left. A small armchair near fire. One small window at Back. A pane of this window is starred by the entrance of a bullet. Under the window to the Right is* 12 *an oak coffin standing on two kitchen chairs. Near the* 13 *coffin is a home-manufactured stool, on which are two lighted candles. Beside the window is a worn-out dresser on which is a small quantity of delf. Tattered remains of cheap lace curtains drape the window. Standing near the window on Left is a brass standard-lamp with a fancy shade; hanging on the wall near the same window is a vividly crimson silk dress, both of which have been looted. A door on Left leading to the bedroom. Another opposite giving a way to the rest of the house. To the Left of this door a common washstand. A tin kettle, very black, and an old saucepan inside the fender. There is no light in the room but that given from the two candles and the fire. The dusk has well fallen, and the glare of the burning buildings in the town can be seen through the window, in the distant sky.* The Covey *and* Fluther *have been playing cards, sitting on the floor by the light of the candles on the stool near the coffin. When the curtain rises* The Covey *is shuffling the cards,* Peter *is sitting in a stiff, dignified way beside him, and* Fluther *is kneeling beside the window, cautiously looking out. It is a few days later.*

Fluther (*furtively peeping out of the window*). Give them a good shuffling. . . . Th' sky's gettin' reddher an' 36 reddher. . . . You'd think it was afire. . . . Half o' th' city must be burnin'.

(6) *air of poverty bordering on destitution:* Bessie's living quarters are even more threadbare and squalid than Nora's two rooms.

(12) *starred by the entrance of a bullet:* a stray bullet has passed through Bessie's window.

(13) *an oak coffin:* Fluther tells us a little later that Mollser and Nora's dead baby are in the coffin.

(36) *a good shuffling:* referring to the playing-cards.

The Covey. If I was you, Fluther, I'd keep away from that window. . . . It's dangerous, an', besides, if they see you, you'll only bring a nose on th' house.   41

Peter. Yes; an' he knows we had to leave our own place th' way they were riddlin' it with machine-gun fire. . . . He'll keep on pimpin' an' pimpin' there, till we have to   44 fly out o' this place too.

Fluther (*ironically*). If they make any attack here, we'll send you out in your green an' glory uniform, shakin' your sword over your head, an' they'll fly before you as th' Danes flew before Brian Boru!   49

The Covey (*placing the cards on the floor, after shuffling them*). Come on, an' cut.
　　　　[Fluther *comes over, sits on floor, and cuts the cards.*

The Covey (*having dealt the cards*). Spuds up again.   54
　　　　　　　　[Nora *moans feebly in room on Left.*

Fluther. There, she's at it again. She's been quiet for a long time, all th' same.

The Covey. She was quiet before, sure, an' she broke out again worse than ever. . . . What was led that time?   59

Peter. Thray o' Hearts, Thray o' Hearts, Thray o' Hearts.   60

Fluther. It's damned hard lines to think of her dead-born   61 kiddie lyin' there in th' arms o' poor little Mollser. Mollser snuffed it sudden too, afther all.

The Covey. Sure she never got any care. How could she get it, an' th' mother out day an' night lookin' for work, an' her consumptive husband leavin' her with a baby to be born before he died!

Voices in a lilting chant to the Left in a distant street. Red Cr . . . oss, Red Cr . . . oss! . . . Ambu . . . lance, Ambu . . . lance!

(41)　*you'll only bring a nose on th' house: the English soldiers will come up to search the house.*

(44)　*pimpin': peeping; Fluther is watching out through the window.*

(49)　*th' Danes flew before Brian Boru: when Brian Bórú beat the Vikings at Clontarf in 1014.*

(54)　*Spuds up: One of the card suits, probably spades, are trumps.*

(59)　*What was led?: which card was placed down first?*

(60)　*Thray o' Hearts[three of hearts]: they are probably playing 'twenty-five'.*

(61)　*hard lines to think: difficult to think of Mollser and the dead baby in the coffin.*

The Covey (*to* Fluther). Your deal, Fluther.

Fluther (*shuffling and dealing the cards*). It'll take a lot out o' Nora—if she'll ever be th' same.

The Covey. Th' docthor thinks she'll never be th' same; thinks she'll be a little touched here. (*He touches his forehead.*) She's ramblin' a lot; thinkin' she's out in th' counthry with Jack; or gettin' his dinner ready for him before he comes home; or yellin' for her kiddie. All that, though, might be th' chloroform she got. . . . I don't know what we'd have done only for oul' Bessie: up with her for th' past three nights, hand runnin'.

Fluther. I always knew there was never anything really derogatory wrong with poor oul' Bessie. (*To* Peter, *who is taking a trick*) Ay, houl' on, there, don't be so damn quick—that's my thrick.

Peter. What's your thrick? It's my thrick, man.

Fluther (*loudly*). How is it your thrick?

Peter (*answering as loudly*). Didn't I lead th' deuce!

Fluther. You must be gettin' blind, man; don't you see th' ace?

Bessie (*appearing at door of room, Left; in a tense whisper*). D'ye want to waken her again on me, when she's just gone asleep? If she wakes will yous come an' mind her? If I hear a whisper out o' one o' yous again, I'll . . . gut yous!

The Covey (*in a whisper*). S-s-s-h. She can hear anything above a whisper.

Peter (*looking up at the ceiling*). Th' gentle an' merciful God 'll give th' pair o' yous a scawldin' an' a scarifyin' one o' these days!

[Fluther *takes a bottle of whisky from his pocket, and takes a drink.*

(79) **might be th' chloroform:** Chloroform, a pain-killing drug, tends to cause hallucinations after prolonged use; but we know from Act III that Nora's mental state was beginning to deteriorate.

(80) **only for oul' Bessie:** Bessie has been with Nora throughout her illness, three days and three nights without a break.

(81) **hand runnin':** in a row.

(85) **that's my thrick:** I won that hand.

(88) **deuce:** two.

(95) **gut yous:** as in gutting a fish.

(99) **th' pair o' yous:** Fluther and The Covey.

(99) **scawldin' an' a scarifyin':** a scolding and a fright.

The Covey (*to* Fluther). Why don't you spread that out, 103 man, an' thry to keep a sup for to-morrow?

Fluther. Spread it out? Keep a sup for to-morrow? How th' hell does a fella know there'll be any to-morrow? If I'm goin' to be whipped away, let me be whipped away 107 when it's empty, an' not when it's half full! (*To* Bessie, *who has seated herself in an armchair at the fire*) How is she, now, Bessie?

Bessie. I left her sleeping quietly. When I'm listenin' to her babblin', I think she'll never be much betther than she is. Her eyes have a hauntin' way of lookin' in instead of lookin' out, as if her mind had been lost alive in madly minglin' memories of th' past. . . . (*Sleepily*) 115 Crushin' her thoughts . . . together . . . in a fierce . . . an' fanciful . . . (*she nods her head and starts wakefully*) idea that dead things are livin', an' livin' things are dead. . . . (*With a start*) Was that a scream I heard her 119 give? (*Reassured*) Blessed God, I think I hear her screamin' every minute! An' it's only there with me that 121 I'm able to keep awake.

The Covey. She'll sleep, maybe, for a long time, now. Ten there.

Fluther. Ten here. If she gets a long sleep, she might be all right. Peter's th' lone five.

The Covey. Whisht! I think I hear somebody movin' below. Whoever it is, he's comin' up.
    [*A pause. Then the door opens and* Captain Brennan *comes into the room. He has changed his uniform for a suit of civvies. His eyes droop* 131 *with the heaviness of exhaustion; his face is pallid and drawn. His clothes are dusty and stained here and there with mud. He leans heavily on the back of a chair as he stands.*

Capt. Brennan. Mrs. Clitheroe; where's Mrs. Clitheroe? I was told I'd find her here.

(103) *spread that out: make it last longer.*
(107) *whipped away: killed.*
(115) *Sleepily: Bessie is obviously exhausted.*
(119) *Was that a scream . . . : Though Bessie can barely keep awake, she wakes constantly, thinking Nora is calling.*
(121) *only there with me: I'm barely able to stay awake.*
(131) *civvies: Brennan has changed into civilian clothes.*

Bessie
  'Her eyes have a hauntin' way of lookin' in instead of lookin' out . . .' (Act IV, lines 113-4)

Nora
  'Something ails me, something ails me. . . . Don't kiss me like that; you take my breath away, Jack.' (Act IV, lines 188-90)

Bessie. What d'ye want with Mrs. Clitheroe?

Capt. Brennan. I've a message, a last message for her from her husband.

Bessie. Killed! He's not killed, is he?

Capt. Brennan (*sinking stiffly and painfully on to a chair*). In th' Imperial Hotel; we fought till th' place was in flames. He was shot through th' arm, an' then through th' lung. . . . I could do nothin' for him—only watch his breath comin' an' goin' in quick, jerky gasps, an' a tiny sthream o' blood thricklin' out of his mouth, down over his lower lip. . . . I said a prayer for th' dyin', an' twined his Rosary beads around his fingers. . . . Then I had to leave him to save meself. . . . (*He shows some holes in his coat*) Look at th' way a machine-gun tore at me coat, as I belted out o' th' buildin' an' darted across th' sthreet for shelter. . . . An' then, I seen The Plough an' th' Stars fallin' like a shot as th' roof crashed in, an' where I'd left poor Jack was nothin' but a leppin' spout o' flame!

Bessie (*with partly repressed vehemence*). Ay, you left him! You twined his Rosary beads round his fingers, an' then you run like a hare to get out o' danger!

Capt. Brennan. I took me chance as well as him. . . . He took it like a man. His last whisper was to "Tell Nora to be brave; that I'm ready to meet my God, an' that I'm proud to die for Ireland." An' when our General heard it he said that "Commandant Clitheroe's end was a gleam of glory." Mrs. Clitheroe's grief will be a joy when she realizes that she has had a hero for a husband.

Bessie. If you only seen her, you'd know to th' differ.
    [Nora *appears at door, Left. She is clad only in her nightdress; her hair, uncared for some days, is hanging in disorder over her shoulders. Her pale face looks paler still because of a vivid red spot on the tip of each cheek. Her eyes are glimmering with the light of incipient in-*

(152) *belted out: ran out.*
(156) *An' then, I seen . . . spout o' flame: Symbolically, the flag falls as Clitheroe dies.*
(167) *you'd know to th' differ: you would change your mind.*
(168) *She is clad only in . . . : Nora's behaviour in this act strongly resembles that of the mad Ophelia in Shakespeare's* Hamlet. *(See the Introduction, page 16).*

130

sanity; her hands are nervously fiddling with 174
her nightgown. She halts at the door for a
moment, looks vacantly around the room, and
then comes slowly in. The rest do not notice her
till she speaks.

Nora (*in a quiet and monotonous tone*). No. . . . Not there,
Jack. . . . I can feel comfortable only in our own 180
familiar place beneath th' bramble tree. . . . We must be
walking for a long time; I feel very, very tired. . . . Have
we to go farther, or have we passed it by? (*Passing her
hand across her eyes*) Curious mist on my eyes. . . . Why
don't you hold my hand, Jack. . . . (*Excitedly*) No, no,
Jack, it's not. Can't you see it's a goldfinch. Look at th'
black-satiny wings with th' gold bars, an' th' splash of
crimson on its head. . . . (*Wearily*). Something ails me,
something ails me. . . . Don't kiss me like that; you take
my breath away, Jack. . . . Why do you frown at me? . . .
You're going away, and (*frightened*) I can't follow you. 191
Something's keeping me from moving. . . . (*Crying out*)
Jack, Jack, Jack!

Bessie (*who has gone over and caught* Nora's *arm*). Now,
Mrs. Clitheroe, you're a terrible woman to get up out of
bed. . . . You'll get cold if you stay here in them clothes.

Nora. Cold? I'm feelin' very cold; it's chilly out here in th'
counthry. . . . (*Looking around frightened*) What place
is this? Where am I?

Bessie (*coaxingly*). You're all right, Nora; you're with
friends, an' in a safe place. Don't you know your uncle
an' your cousin, an' poor oul' Fluther?

Peter (*about to go over to* Nora). Nora, darlin', now—

Fluther (*pulling him back*). Now, leave her to Bessie,
man. A crowd 'll only make her worse.

Nora (*thoughtfully*). There is something I want to remember, an' I can't. (*With agony*) I can't, I can't, I can't!
My head, my head! (*Suddenly breaking from* Bessie,

(174) *incipient insanity: the early
stages of insanity.*

(180) *Not there, Jack: Nora believes
she is walking in the
countryside with Clitheroe.*

(191) *I can't follow you: a mixture
of reality and fantasy; Nora
sees Clitheroe leaving and
knows she cannot follow,
although she has not been
told of his death.*

and running over to the men, and gripping Fluther *by the shoulders*) Where is it? Where's my baby? Tell me where you've put it, where've you hidden it? My baby, my baby; I want my baby! My head, my poor head. . . . Oh, I can't tell what is wrong with me. (*Screaming*) Give him to me, give me my husband!

Bessie. Blessin' o' God on us, isn't this pitiful!

Nora (*struggling with* Bessie). I won't go away for you; I won't. Not till you give me back my husband. (*Screaming*) Murderers, that's what yous are; murderers, murderers!

Bessie. S-s-sh. We'll bring Mr. Clitheroe back to you, if you'll only lie down an' stop quiet. . . . (*Trying to lead her in*) Come on, now, Nora, an' I'll sing something to you.

Nora. I feel as if my life was thryin' to force its way out of my body. . . . I can hardly breathe . . . I'm frightened, I'm frightened, I'm frightened! For God's sake, don't leave me, Bessie. Hold my hand, put your arms around me!

Fluther (*to* Brennan). Now you can see th' way she is, man. 229

Peter. An' what way would she be if she heard Jack had gone west? 231

The Covey (*to* Peter). Shut up, you, man!

Bessie (*to* Nora). We'll have to be brave, an' let patience clip away th' heaviness of th' slow-movin' hours, re- 234 memberin' that sorrow may endure for th' night, but joy cometh in th' mornin'. . . . Come on in, an' I'll sing to you, an' you'll rest quietly.

Nora (*stopping suddenly on her way to the room*). Jack an' me are goin' out somewhere this evenin'. Where I can't tell. Isn't it curious I can't remember. . . . Maura, Maura, Jack, if th' baby's a girl; any name you like, if th'

(229) *Now you can see . . . : Brennan cannot answer; Nora's insanity has made a mockery of all his talk of grief becoming joy.*

(231) *gone west: been killed.*

(234) *let patience clip away . . . : only patience can help pass the long hours of grief.*

baby's a boy! . . . He's there. (*Screaming*) He's there, an' they won't give him back to me!

Bessie. S-ss-s-h, darlin', s-ssh. I won't sing to you, if you're not quiet.

Nora (*nervously holding* Bessie). Hold my hand, hold my hand, an' sing to me, sing to me!

Bessie. Come in an' lie down, an' I'll sing to you.

Nora (*vehemently*). Sing to me, sing to me; sing, sing!

Bessie (*singing as she leads* Nora *into room*):

> Lead, kindly light, amid th' encircling gloom, 251
> Lead Thou me on.
> Th' night is dark an' I am far from home,
> Lead Thou me on.
> Keep Thou my feet, I do not ask to see
> Th' distant scene—one step enough for me.
>
> So long that Thou hast blessed me, sure Thou still
> Wilt lead me on;   [*They go in.*

Bessie (*singing in room*):

> O'er moor an' fen, o'er crag an' torrent, till
> Th' night is gone.
> An' in th' morn those angel faces smile
> That I have lov'd long since, an' lost awhile!

The Covey (*to* Brennan). Now that you've seen how bad she is, an' that we daren't tell her what has happened till she's betther, you'd best be slippin' back to where you come from.

Capt. Brennan. There's no chance o' slippin' back now, for th' military are everywhere: a fly couldn't get through. I'd never have got here, only I managed to change me uniform for what I'm wearin'. . . . I'll have to take me chance, an' thry to lie low here for a while.

---

(251) *'Lead, Kindly Light': an Anglican hymn.*

The Covey (*frightened*). There's no place here to lie low. 273
Th' Tommies 'll be hoppin' in here, any minute!

Peter (*aghast*). An' then we'd all be shanghaied! 275

The Covey. Be God, there's enough afther happenin' to us!

Fluther (*warningly, as he listens*). Whisht, whisht, th'
whole o' yous. I think I heard th' clang of a rifle butt on
th' floor of th' hall below. (*All alertness.*) Here, come on
with th' cards again. I'll deal.
[*He shuffles and deals the cards to all.*

Fluther. Clubs up. (*To* Brennan) Thry to keep your hands
from shakin', man. You lead, Peter. (*As* Peter *throws
out a card*) Four o' Hearts led.
[*The door opens and* Corporal Stoddart *of the
Wiltshires enters in full war kit; steel helmet,
rifle and bayonet, and trench tool. He looks
round the room. A pause and a palpable* 288
silence.

Fluther (*breaking the silence*). Two tens an' a five.

Corporal Stoddart. 'Ello. (*Indicating the coffin*) This the
stiff? 292

The Covey. Yis.

Corporal Stoddart. Who's gowing with it? Ownly one 294
allowed to gow with it, you know.

The Covey. I dunno.

Corporal Stoddart. You dunnow?

The Covey. I dunno.

Bessie (*coming into the room*). She's afther slippin' off to
sleep again, thanks be to God. I'm hardly able to keep
me own eyes open. (*To the soldier*) Oh, are yous goin' to
take away poor little Mollser?

(273) *There's no place here: The
Covey fears being implicated
in the fighting if Brennan is
found with them.*

(275) *shanghaied: See the note to
line 108 in Act III.*

(288) *palpable: that can be touched
or felt.*

(292) *This the stiff?: The British
army would have been
informed of Mollser's death
since they would need to
escort the coffin to the
cemetery.*

(294) *gowing [going]: the soldiers
speak with Cockney accents.*

Corporal Stoddart. Ay; 'oo's agowing with 'er? 303

Bessie. Oh, th' poor mother, o' course. God help her, it's a terrible blow to her!

Fluther. A terrible blow? Sure, she's in her element now, 306 woman, mixin' earth to earth, an' ashes t'ashes an' dust to dust, an' revellin' in plumes an' hearses, last days an' judgements!

Bessie (*falling into chair by the fire*). God bless us! I'm jaded!

Corporal Stoddart. Was she plugged?

The Covey. Ah, no; died o' consumption.

Corporal Stoddart. Ow, is that all? Thought she moight 314 'ave been plugged.

The Covey. Is that all? Isn't it enough? D'ye know, comrade, that more die o' consumption than are killed in th' wars? An' it's all because of th' system we're livin' undher? 319

Corporal Stoddart. Ow, I know. I'm a Sowcialist moiself, but I 'as to do my dooty. 321

The Covey (*ironically*). Dooty! Th' only dooty of a Socialist is th' emancipation of th' workers.

Corporal Stoddart. Ow, a man's a man, an 'e 'as to foight for 'is country, 'asn't 'e?

Fluther (*aggressively*). You're not fightin' for your counthry here, are you? 327

Peter (*anxiously, to* Fluther). Ay, ay, Fluther, none o' that, none o' that!

The Covey. Fight for your counthry! Did y'ever read, comrade, Jenersky's *Thesis on the Origin, Develop-*

(303) 'oo's agowing?: who is going?
(306) she's in her element . . . : Because Mrs. Gogan attaches such great importance to death, she would actually feel a death in the family to be something of an honour. O'Casey later confirms this: see lines 348-350.
(314) moight [might].
(319) th' system we're livin' undher: the capitalist system.
(321) I 'as to [I have to].
(321) dooty [duty].
(327) You're not . . . are you?: a very relevant question, and one that the soldier cannot answer.

ment, an' Consolidation of th' Evolutionary Idea of the Proletariat?

Corporal Stoddart. Ow, cheese it, Paddy, cheese it! 334

Bessie (*sleepily*). How is things in th' town, Tommy?

Corporal Stoddart. Ow, I fink it's nearly hover. We've got 336
'em surrounded, and we're clowsing in on the
bloighters. Ow, it was only a little bit of a dawgfight. 338
[*The sharp ping of the sniper's rifle is heard,
followed by a squeal of pain.*

Voices to the Left in a chant. Red Cr . . . oss, Red Cr . . . oss!
Ambu . . . lance, Ambu . . . lance!

Corporal Stoddart (*excitedly*). Christ, that's another of
our men 'it by that blawsted sniper! 'E's knocking abaht
'ere, somewheres. Gawd, when we gets th' bloighter, 345
we'll give 'im the cold steel, we will. We'll jab the belly
aht of 'im, we will!
[Mrs. Gogan *comes in tearfully, and a little proud* 348
*of the importance of being directly connected
with death.*

Mrs. Gogan (*to* Fluther). I'll never forget what you done
for me, Fluther, goin' around at th' risk of your life
settlin' everything with th' undhertaker an' th' cemetery
people. When all me own were afraid to put their noses
out, you plunged like a good one through hummin'
bullets, an' they knockin' fire out o' th' road, tinklin'
through th' frightened windows, an' splashin'
themselves to pieces on th' walls! An' you'll find, that
Mollser, in th' happy place she's gone to, won't forget to
whisper, now an' again, th' name o' Fluther.

Corporal Stoddart. Git it aht, mother, git it aht. 361

Bessie (*from the chair*). It's excusin' me you'll be, Mrs.
Gogan, for not stannin' up, seein' I'm shaky on me feet
for want of a little sleep, an' not desirin' to show any
disrespect to poor little Mollser.

(334) cheese it: stop it.
(336) hover [over].
(338) a dawg fight [a dog-fight].
*(345) bloighter [blighter]: an
annoying or contemptible
person.*
*(348) a little proud: See note to line
306 above.*
*(361) Git it aht: Stoddart wants
Mrs. Gogan to have the coffin
moved.*

Corporal Stoddart
  'I'm a Sowcialist moiself, but I 'as to do my dooty.' (Act IV, lines 320-1)

Bessie
  'Jesus Christ, me sight's goin'! It's all dark, dark!' (Act IV, lines 610-11)

Fluther. Sure, we all know, Bessie, that it's vice versa with you.

Mrs. Gogan (*to* Bessie). Indeed, it's meself that has well chronicled, Mrs. Burgess, all your gentle hurryin's to me little Mollser, when she was alive, bringin' her somethin' to dhrink, or somethin' t'eat, an' never passin' her without liftin' up her heart with a delicate word o' kindness. ₃₆₉

Corporal Stoddart (*impatiently, but kindly*). Git it aht, git it aht, mother. ₃₇₄

[The Covey, Fluther, Brennan, *and* Peter *carry out the coffin, followed by* Mrs. Gogan.

Corporal Stoddart (*to* Bessie, *who is almost asleep*). 'Ow many men is in this 'ere 'ouse? (*No answer. Loudly*) 'Ow many men is in this 'ere 'ouse? ₃₈₀

Besie (*waking with a start*). God, I was nearly asleep! . . . How many men? Didn't you see them?

Corporal Stoddart. Are they all that are in the 'ouse?

Bessie. Oh, there's none higher up, but there may be more lower down. Why?

Corporal Stoddart. All men in the district 'as to be rounded up. Somebody's giving 'elp to the snipers, and we 'as to take precautions. If I 'ad my woy, I'd make 'em all join hup, and do their bit! But I suppowse they and you are all Shinners. ₃₈₈ ₃₈₉ ₃₉₀

Bessie (*who has been sinking into sleep, waking up to a sleepy vehemence*). Bessie Burgess is no Shinner, an' never had no thruck with anything spotted be th' fingers o' th' Fenians; but always made it her business to harness herself for Church whenever she knew that God Save the King was goin' to be sung at th' end of th' service; whose only son went to th' front in th' first contingent of the Dublin Fusiliers, an' that's on his way home carryin' a shatthered arm that he got fightin' for ₃₉₃ ₃₉₄ ₃₉₅ ₃₉₆ ₃₉₉

(369) *chronicled: as in keeping a record of something in writing.*

(374) *impatiently, but kindly: As we can see from this stage direction, O'Casey does not try to portray the English soldiers as being callous or cruel.*

(380) *'Ow many [How many].*

(388) *'ad my woy [I had my way].*

(389) *make 'em all join hup: Conscription for the British army during the First World War was not extended to Ireland.*

(390) *Shinner: a member of Sinn Féin or the Irish Volunteers.*

(393) *no thruck with: nothing to do with.*

(394) *spotted be th' fingers o': connected with and soiled by.*

(395) *harness herself: prepare herself for.*

(396) *God Save . . . th' service: In other words, a Protestant service.*

(399) *shatthered arm: This is the only mention Bessie ever makes of her son being injured.*

his King an' counthry!

[*Her head sinks slowly forward again.* Peter ₄₀₁ *comes into the room; his body is stiffened and his face is wearing a comically indignant look. He walks to and fro at the back of the room, evidently repressing a violent desire to speak angrily. He is followed in by* Fluther, The Covey, *and* Brennan, *who slinks into an obscure corner of the room, nervous of notice.*

Fluther (*after an embarrassing pause*). Th' air in th' sthreet outside's shakin' with the firin' o' rifles an' machine-guns. It must be a hot shop in th' middle o' th' scrap. ₄₁₂

Corporal Stoddart. We're pumping lead in on 'em from ₄₁₃ every side, now; they'll soon be shoving up th' white flag.

Peter (*with a shout*). I'm tellin' you either o' yous two lowsers 'ud make a betther hearse-man than Peter; proddin' an' pokin' at me an' I helpin' to carry out a corpse!

Fluther. It wasn't a very derogatory thing for Th' Covey to ₄₂₀ say that you'd make a fancy hearse-man, was it?

Peter (*furiously*). A pair o' redjesthered bowseys ₄₂₂ pondherin' from mornin' till night on how they'll get a ₄₂₃ chance to break a gap through th' quiet nature of a man that's always endeavourin' to chase out of him any sthray thought of venom against his fella-man! ₄₂₆

The Covey. Oh, shut it, shut it, shut it!

Peter. As long as I'm a livin' man, responsible for me thoughts, words, an' deeds to th' Man above, I'll feel ₄₂₉ meself instituted to fight again' th' sliddherin' ways of a ₄₃₀ pair o' picaroons, whisperin', concurrin', concoctin', ₄₃₁ an' conspirin' together to rendher me unconscious of ₄₃₂ th' life I'm thryin' to live!

(401) *Her head sinks:* Bessie falls back to sleep.
(412) *a hot shop . . . th' scrap:* The fighting, especially in O'Connell Street, is drawing to a climax.
(413) *pumping lead:* firing.
(420) *It wasn't a . . . :* It seems that while carrying the coffin, The Covey said Peter would make a good hearse-man. Peter is not amused.
(422) *redjesthered bowseys:* registered hooligans.
(423) *pondherin'* [*pondering*]: thinking over.
(426) *th' quiet nature . . . his fella-man:* As in Act I, Peter maintains that although he is by nature a quiet man, people are forever trying to aggravate him.
(429) *th' Man above:* God in Heaven.
(430) *instituted:* obliged.
(431) *picaroons:* rogues.
(432) *rendher me unconscious of:* cause me to forget.

Corporal Stoddart (*dumbfounded*). What's wrong, Daddy; wot 'ave they done to you?

Peter (*savagely to the* Corporal). You mind your own business! What's it got to do with you, what's wrong with me?

Bessie (*in a sleepy murmur*). Will yous thry to conthrol yourselves into quietness? Yous'll waken her . . . up . . . on . . . me . . . again.   [*She sleeps.*

Fluther. Come on, boys, to th' cards again, an' never mind him.

Corporal Stoddart. No use of you gowing to start cawds; you'll be gowing out of 'ere, soon as Sergeant comes.

Fluther. Goin' out o' here? An' why're we goin' out o' here?

Corporal Stoddart. All men in district to be rounded up, and 'eld in till the scrap is hover.   448

Fluther. An' where're we goin' to be held in?

Corporal Stoddart. They're puttin' 'em in a church.

The Covey. A church?

Fluther. What sort of a church? Is it a Protestan' Church?

Corporal Stoddart. I dunnow; I suppowse so.

Fluther (*dismayed*). Be God, it'll be a nice thing to be stuck   454
all night in a Protestan' Church!

Corporal Stoddart. Bring the cawds; you moight get a chance of a goime.   457

Fluther. Ah, no, that wouldn't do. . . . I wondher? (*After a moment's thought*) Ah, I don't think we'd be doin' anything derogatory be playin' cards in a Protestan' Church.   461

(448) *'eld in till the scrap is hover: They are to be held captive until the fighting is over. O'Casey himself was subjected to this during the rising.*

(454) *dismayed: As a Catholic, Fluther is upset by the idea of having to spend any amount of time in a Protestant church.*

(457) *goime [game].*

(461) *I don't think . . . Protestan' Church: Because it is a Protestant church, Fluther feels that playing cards there would not be a sacrilege.*

Corporal Stoddart. If I was you I'd bring a little snack with me; you moight be glad of it before the mawning. ₄₆₃ (*Sings*):

I do loike a snoice mince poy, ₄₆₅
I do loike a snoice mince poy!
[*The snap of the sniper's rifle rings out again, followed simultaneously by a scream of pain. Corporal Stoddart goes pale, and brings his rifle to the ready, listening.*

Voices chanting to the Right. Red Cro . . . ss, Red Cro . . . ss! Ambu . . . lance, Ambu . . . lance!
[*Sergeant Tinley comes rapidly in, pale, agitated, and fiercely angry.*

Corporal Stoddart (*to* Sergeant). One of hour men 'it, Sergeant?

Sergeant Tinley. Private Taylor; got 'it roight through the ₄₇₇ chest, 'e did; an 'ole in front of 'im as 'ow you could put your fist through, and 'arf 'is back blown awoy! ₄₇₉ Dum-dum bullets they're using. Gang of Hassassins ₄₈₀ potting at us from behind roofs. That's not playing the goime: why down't they come into the owpen and ₄₈₂ foight fair!

Fluther (*unable to stand the slight*). Fight fair! A few hundhred scrawls o' chaps with a couple o' guns an' ₄₈₅ Rosary beads, again' a hundhred thousand thrained ₄₈₆ men with horse, fut, an' artillery . . . an' he wants us to fight fair? (*To* Sergeant) D'ye want us to come out in our skins an' throw stones?

Sergeant Tinley (*to* Corporal). Are these four all that are 'ere?

Corporal Stoddart. Four; that's all, Sergeant.

Sergeant Tinley (*vindictively*). Come on, then; get the blighters aht. (*To the men*) 'Ere, 'op it aht! Aht into the streets with you, and if a snioper sends another of our

141

(463) *mawning* [*morning*].

(465) *snoice* [*nice*].

(477) *Private Taylor: To balance the tragic death of Clitheroe, O'Casey gives us a quick glimpse of things from the English perspective. The mention of the soldier's name personalises him to a degree and helps us to sympathise with him.*

(479) *an 'ole . . . awoy* [a hole in his front that you could put your fist through and half his back blown away].

(480) *Dum-dum bullets: soft-topped lead bullets that explode on impact, causing great internal damage to their victims; such bullets were not in fact used by the Volunteers or Citizen Army.*

(480) *Hassassins* [*assassins*]: *paid killers.*

(482) *not playing the goime: identical to Fluther's words in Act III: neither side believes the other to be fighting fairly.*

(485) *scrawls o' chaps with a couple o' guns: the poorly trained, poorly armed men of the Citizen Army and Volunteers.*

(486) *again'* [*against*]: *versus.*

men west, you gow with 'im! (*He catches* Fluther *by the shoulder*) Gow on, git aht!

Fluther. Eh, who are you chuckin', eh?   498

Sergeant Tinley (*roughly*). Gow on, git aht, you blighter.

Fluther. Who are you callin' a blighter to, eh? I'm a Dublin man, born an' bred in th' city, see?

Sergeant Tinley. I down't care if you were Broin Buroo;   502
git aht, git aht.

Fluther (*halting as he is going out*). Jasus, you an' your guns! Leave them down, an' I'd beat th' two o' yous without sweatin'!

> [Peter, Brennan, The Covey, *and* Fluther, *followed by the soldiers, go out.* Bessie *is sleeping heavily on the chair by the fire. After a pause,* Nora *appears at door, Left, in her nightdress. Remaining at door for a few moments she looks vaguely around the room. She then comes in quietly, goes over to the fire, pokes it, and puts the kettle on. She thinks for a few moments, pressing her hand to her forehead. She looks questioningly at the fire, and then at the press at back. She goes to the press, opens it, takes out a soiled cloth and spreads it on the table. She then places things for tea on the table.*

Nora. I imagine th' room looks very odd somehow. . . . I was nearly forgetting Jack's tea. . . . Ah, I think I'll have everything done before he gets in. . . . (*She lilts gently, as she arranges the table*).

> Th' violets were scenting th' woods, Nora,   525
>   Displaying their charms to th' bee,
> When I first said I lov'd only you, Nora,
>   An' you said you lov'd only me.
>
> Th' chestnut blooms gleam'd through th' glade,
>   Nora,

(498) *chuckin': pushing.*
(502) *Broin Buroo [Brian Bórú].*
(525) *Th' violets were . . . : the song Clitheroe sang to Nora in Act I.*

142

A robin sang loud from a tree,
When I first said I lov'd only you, Nora,
An' you said you lov'd only me.
[*She pauses suddenly, and glances round the room.*

Nora (*doubtfully*). I can't help feelin' this room very strange. . . . What is it? . . . What is it? . . . I must think. . . . I must thry to remember. . . .

Voices chanting in a distant street. Ambu . . . lance, Ambu . . . lance! Red Cro . . . ss, Red Cro . . . ss!

Nora (*startled and listening for a moment, then resuming the arrangement of the table*):

Trees, birds, an' bees sang a song, Nora,
Of happier transports to be,
When I first said I lov'd only you, Nora,
An' you said you lov'd only me.

[*A burst of rifle fire is heard in a street near by, followed by the rapid tok, tok, tok of a machine-gun.*

Nora (*staring in front of her and screamin*). Jack, Jack, Jack! My baby, my baby, my baby!

Bessie (*waking with a start*). You divil, are you afther gettin' out o' bed again!
[*She rises and runs towards* Nora, *who rushes to the window, which she frantically opens.*

Nora (*at window, screaming*). Jack, Jack, for God's sake, come to me!

Soldiers (*outside, shouting*). Git away, git away from that window, there!

Bessie (*seizing hold of* Nora). Come away, come away, woman, from that window!

Nora (*struggling with* Bessie). Where is it; where have you hidden it? Oh, Jack, Jack, where are you?

Bessie (*imploringly*). Mrs. Clitheroe, for God's sake, come away!

Nora (*fiercely*). I won't; he's below. Let . . . me . . . go! You're thryin' to keep me from me husband. I'll follow him. Jack, Jack, come to your Nora!

Bessie. Hus-s-sh, Nora, Nora! He'll be here in a minute. I'll bring him to you, if you'll only be quiet—honest to God, I will.

> [*With a great effort* Bessie *pushes* Nora *away from the window, the force used causing her to stagger against it herself. Two rifle shots ring out in quick succession.* Bessie *jerks her body convulsively; stands stiffly for a moment, a look of agonized astonishment on her face, then she staggers forward, leaning heavily on the table with her hands.*

Bessie (*with an arrested scream of fear and pain*). Merciful God, I'm shot, I'm shot, I'm shot! . . . Th' life's pourin' out o' me! (*To* Nora) I've got this through . . . through you . . . through you, you bitch, you! . . . O God, have mercy on me! . . . (*To* Nora) You wouldn't stop quiet, no, you wouldn't, you wouldn't, blast you! Look at what I'm afther gettin', look at what I'm afther gettin' . . . I'm bleedin' to death, an' no one's here to stop th' flowin' blood! (*Calling*) Mrs. Gogan, Mrs. Gogan! Fluther, Fluther, for God's sake, somebody, a doctor, a doctor!

> [*She staggers frightened towards the door, to seek for aid, but, weakening half-way across the room, she sinks to her knees, and bending forward, supports herself with her hands resting on the floor.* Nora *is standing rigidly with her back to the wall opposite, her trembling hands held out a little from the sides of her body, her lips quivering, her breast heaving, staring wildly at the figure of* Bessie.

Nora (*in a breathless whisper*). Jack, I'm frightened. . . . I'm frightened, Jack. . . . Oh, Jack, where are you?

Bessie (*moaningly*). This is what's afther comin' on me for nursin' you day an' night. . . . I was a fool, a fool, a fool! Get me a dhrink o' wather, you jade, will you? There's a ⁶⁰³ fire burnin' in me blood! (*Pleadingly*) Nora, Nora, dear, for God's sake, run out an' get Mrs. Gogan, or Fluther, or somebody to bring a doctor, quick, quick, quick! (*As* Nora *does not stir*) Blast you, stir yourself, before I'm gone!

Nora. Oh, Jack, Jack, where are you?

Bessie (*in a whispered moan*). Jesus Christ, me sight's goin'! It's all dark, dark! Nora, hold me hand!
[Bessie's *body lists over and she sinks into a prostrate position on the floor.*

Bessie. I'm dyin', I'm dyin' . . . I feel it. . . . Oh God, oh God! (*She feebly sings*)

> I do believe, I will believe
>   That Jesus died for me;
> That on th' cross He shed His blood,
>   From sin to set me free. . . .

> I do believe . . . I will believe
>   . . . Jesus died . . . me;
> . . . th' cross He shed . . . blood,
>   From sin . . . free.

[*She ceases singing, and lies stretched out, still and very rigid. A pause. Then* Mrs. Gogan *runs hastily in.*

Mrs. Gogan (*quivering with fright*). Blessed be God, what's afther happenin'? (*To* Nora) What's wrong, child, what's wrong? (*She sees* Bessie, *runs to her and bends over the body*) Bessie, Bessie! (*She shakes the body*) Mrs. Burgess, Mrs. Burgess! (*She feels* Bessie's *forehead*) My God, she's as cold as death. They're afther murdherin' th' poor inoffensive woman!
[Sergeant Tinley *and* Corporal Stoddart *enter agitatedly, their rifles at the ready.*

(603) jade: *an insulting term for a woman.*

Sergeant Tinley (*excitedly*). This is the 'ouse. That's the window!

Nora (*pressing back against the wall*). Hide it, hide it; 638 cover it up, cover it up!

Sergeant Tinley (*going over to the body*). 'Ere, what's this? Who's this? (*Looking at* Bessie) Oh Gawd, we've plugged one of the women of the 'ouse. 642

Corporal Stoddart. Whoy the 'ell did she gow to the window? Is she dead?

Sergeant Tinley. Oh, dead as bedamned. Well, we couldn't afford to toike any chawnces. 646

Nora (*screaming*). Hide it, hide it; don't let me see it! Take me away, take me away, Mrs. Gogan!
    [Mrs. Gogan *runs into room, Left, and runs out again with a sheet which she spreads over the body of* Bessie.

Mrs. Gogan (*as she spreads the sheet*). Oh, God help her, th' poor woman, she's stiffenin' out as hard as she can! Her face has written on it th' shock o' sudden agony, an' her hands is whitenin' into th' smooth shininess of wax.

Nora (*whimperingly*). Take me away, take me away; don't leave me here to be lookin' an' lookin' at it!

Mrs. Gogan (*going over to* Nora *and putting her arm around her*). Come on with me, dear, an' you can doss in 659 poor Mollser's bed, till we gather some neighbours to come an' give th' last friendly touches to Bessie in th' lonely layin' of her out.
    [Mrs. Gogan *and* Nora *go slowly out.*

Corporal Stoddart (*who has been looking around, to* Sergeant Tinley). Tea here, Sergeant. Wot abaht a cup of scald? 666

Sergeant Tinley. Pour it aht, Stoddart, pour it aht. I could

(638) *Hide it: Nora cannot stand the sight of Bessie's dead body.*

(642) *Oh Gawd, we've plugged . . . : The soldiers are themselves shocked by the fact that they have killed a woman.*

(646) *toike any chawnces: They could not afford to take any chances because of snipers.*

(659) *doss: sleep.*

(666) *cup of scald: cup of tea.*

scoff hanything just now.

[*Corporal Stoddart pours out two cups of tea, and the two soldiers begin to drink. In the distance is heard a bitter burst of rifle and machine-gun fire, interspersed with the boom, boom of artillery. The glare in the sky seen through the window flares into a fuller and a deeper red.*]

Sergeant Tinley. There gows the general attack on the Powst Office.

Voices in a distant street. Ambu . . . lance, Ambu . . . lance! Red Cro . . . ss, Red Cro . . . ss!

[*The voices of soldiers at a barricade outside the house are heard singing:*

They were summoned from the 'illside,
They were called in from the glen,
And the country found 'em ready
At the stirring call for men.
Let not tears add to their 'ardship,
As the soldiers pass along,
And although our 'eart is breaking,
Make it sing this cheery song.

Sergeant Tinley and Corporal Stoddart (*joining in the chorus, as they sip the tea*):

Keep the 'owme fires burning,
While your 'earts are yearning;
Though your lads are far away
They dream of owme;
There's a silver loining
Through the dark cloud shoining,
Turn the dark cloud inside out,
Till the boys come 'owme!

CURTAIN

END ACT IV

(668) *scoff*: to eat greedily: here he is referring to the tea they are about to drink.

(676) *There gows . . . the Powst Office*: As the play draws to an end, so too does the rising.

(691) *'Keep the Home Fires Burning'*: the traditional anthem since the First World War of British soldiers fighting far from home.

WORKSHOP ACTIVITIES

WORKSHOP ACTIVITIES FOR ACT I

With just a minimum of preparation, the following sections could be used for dramatised readings (with some amusement) in the class. Each one involves an argument of some description.

Students should keep in mind that most characters do not lose their tempers immediately but do so gradually. For example in section A, Fluther begins by dismissing Mrs. Gogan's words *carelessly*. He then reacts to her story *a little nervously*. Following this, and now quite worried, he speaks *faintly*. Then, convinced that he is about to die, he says in desperation: 'Suddenly gettin' hot an' then, just as suddenly gettin' cold.' Finally, as Mrs. Gogan holds the shroud-like shirt up to him, he can take it no more and his temper is let loose; *vehemently* he shouts, 'Blast you an' your nightshirt . . .' etc.

As you can see, the stage instructions are a very useful guide. In section B, the volume with which Fluther and The Covey speak goes from *rather loudly* to *more loudly* to *loudly*, then to *scornfully*, and on to *fiercely*.

On the other hand, in section C, while the taunting Covey remains calm, Uncle Peter instantly loses his temper. The stage instructions tell us: *Flinging the dungarees violently on the floor.*

In section D, because it is a more complicated scene, there are many stage instructions. For example: *provokingly, decisively, explosively, remonstratively*, and *snappily*, to name but a few. In preparing a reading of this scene it would be wise to get the precise meanings of the words, experiment with the tone of your voice until the two match, and then go over the scene a number of times.

Subsequent class discussion may then prove rewarding. If, for example, two groups do the same section, a comparison of both interpretations can be made on the basis of which one the class prefers, and why.

The sections are as follows:

Section A. From line 223 (Mrs. Gogan): 'Oh, you've got a cold on you, Fluther . . .' to line 265: '. . . shining shroud.'

Section B. From line 312 (Fluther): 'We're all Irishmen . . .' to line 381: '. . . red–flag socialist.'

Section C. From line 410 (Peter): 'Where are you throwin' them . . .' to line 462: '. . . I'll do for you.'

Section D. From line 620 (The Covey): 'Another cut o' bread . . .' to line 692: '. . . marchin' to the meeting.'

WORKSHOP ACTIVITIES FOR ACT II

A useful practical way to highlight the structure and dominant theme of this act is to rearrange some of the speeches. The act consists, essentially, of two separate fights (squabbles would be a more appropriate description), between Bessie and Mrs. Gogan, and between Fluther and The Covey. These fights are punctuated by the Figure in the Window with his fiery oratory. Thus, in order to get to the heart of the act, we can pare it down to these three elements and produce a more concentrated version.

In the following adaptation the arguments are not supposed to be happening at the same time. Bessie and Mrs. Gogan argue, then freeze, while Fluther and The Covey take over; and in between, the Figure in the Window delivers his piece. Neither party is aware of the other's existence. Ultimately, the irony of Act II is made all the more obvious and more accessible, the comedy of the contrasting attitudes more immediate to the student. Each of the characters, including the Figure in the Window, should try to bring out as much *aggression* as possible, the aggression of the words, as well as the emotions.

The Voice of the Man. It is a glorious thing to see arms in the hands of Irishmen. We must accustom ourselves to the thought of arms, we must accustom ourselves to the sight of arms, we must accustom ourselves to the use of arms. . . . Bloodshed is a cleansing and sanctifying thing, and the nation that regards it as the final horror has lost its manhood. . . . There are many things more horrible than bloodshed, and slavery is one of them!

Bessie (*speaking to* The Covey, *but really at the other party*). I can't for th' life o' me undherstand how they can call themselves Catholics, when they won't lift a finger to help poor little Catholic Belgium.

Mrs. Gogan. (*raising her voice*). What about poor little Catholic Ireland?

Bessie (*to* Mrs. Gogan). You mind your own business, ma'am, an' stupefy your foolishness be gettin' dhrunk. . . . There's a storm of anger tossin' in me heart

149

thinkin' of all th' poor Tommies, an' with them me own son, dhrenched in water an' soaked in blood, gropin' their way to a shattherin' death, in a shower o' shells! Young men with th' sunny lust o' life beamin' in them, layin' down their white bodies, shredded into torn an' bloody pieces, on th' althar that God Himself has built for th' sacrifice of heroes!

Mrs. Gogan. Isn't it a nice thing to have to be listenin' to a lassie an' hangin' our heads in a dead silence, knowin' that some persons think more of a ball of malt than they do of th' blessed saints.

Bessie. To look at some o' th' women that's knockin' about, now, is a thing to make a body sigh. . . . A woman on her own, dhrinkin' with a bevy o' men, is hardly an example to her sex. . . . A woman dhrinkin' with a woman is one thing, an' a woman dhrinkin' with herself is still a woman—flappers may be put in another category altogether—but a middle-aged married woman makin' herself th' centre of a circle of men is as a woman that is loud an' stubborn, whose feet abideth not in her own house.

Mrs. Gogan (*dipping her finger in the whisky, and moistening with it the lips of her baby*). Cissie Gogan's a woman livin' for nigh on twenty-five years in her own room, an' beyond biddin' th' time o' day to her neighbours, never yet as much as nodded her head in th' direction of other people's business, while she knows some as are never content unless they're standin' senthry over other people's doin's!

Fluther. Th' meetin' should be soon over, now.

The Covey. Th' sooner th' better. It's all a lot o' blasted nonsense, comrade.

Fluther. Oh, I wouldn't say it was all nonsense. Afther all, Fluther can remember th' time, an' him only a dawny chiselur, bein' taught at his mother's knee to be faithful to th' Shan Van Vok!

150

The Covey. That's all dope, comrade; th' sort o' thing that workers are fed on be th' Boorzwawzee.

Fluther (*a little sharply*). What's all dope? Though I'm sayin' it that shouldn't: (*catching his cheek with his hand, and pulling down the flesh from the eye*) d'ye see that mark there, undher me eye? . . . A sabre slice from a dragoon in O'Connell Street! (*Thrusting his head forward towards* Rosie). Feel that dint in th' middle o' me nut! . . . (*putting on his hat with quiet pride*). A skelp from a bobby's baton at a Labour meetin' in th' Phoenix Park!

The Covey. He must ha' hitten you in mistake. I don't know what you ever done for th' Labour movement.

Fluther (*loudly*). D'ye not? Maybe, then, I done as much, an' know as much about th' Labour movement as th' chancers that are blowin' about it!

The Covey. There's no necessity to get excited about it, comrade.

Fluther (*more loudly*). Excited? Who's gettin' excited? There's no one gettin' excited! It would take something more than a thing like you to flutther a feather o' Fluther. Blatherin', an', when all is said, you know as much as th' rest in th' wind up!

The Covey. Well, let us put it to th' test, then, an' see what you know about th' Labour movement: what's the mechanism of exchange?

Fluther (*roaring, because he feels he is beaten*). How th' hell do I know what it is? There's nothin' about that in th' rules of our Thrades Union!

The Covey. What does Karl Marx say about th' Relation of Value to th' Cost o' Production?

Fluther (*angrily*). What th' hell do I care what he says? I'm

151

Irishman enough not to lose me head be follyin' foreigners!

The Covey. It's only waste o' time talkin' to you, comrade.

Fluther. Don't be comradin' me, mate. I'd be on me last legs if I wanted you for a comrade.

Voice of the Man. Comrade soldiers of the Irish Volunteers and of the Citizen Army, we rejoice in this terrible war. The old heart of the earth needed to be warmed with the red wine of the battlefields. . . . Such august homage was never offered to God as this: the homage of millions of lives given gladly for love of country. And we must be ready to pour out the same red wine in the same glorious sacrifice, for without shedding of blood there is no redemption!

Bessie. They may crow away out o' them; but it ud be fitther for some o' them to mend their ways, an' cease from havin' scouts out watchin' for th' comin' of th' Saint Vincent de Paul man, for fear they'd be nailed lowerin' a pint of beer, mockin' th' man with an angel face, shinin' with th' glamour of deceit an' lies!

Mrs. Gogan. An' a certain lassie standin' stiff behind her own door with her ears cocked listenin' to what's being said, stuffed till she's sthrained with envy of a neighbour thryin' for a few little things that may be got be hard sthrivin' to keep up to th' letter an' th' law, an' th' practices of th' Church!

Bessie. Bessie Burgess doesn't put up to know much, never havin' a swaggerin' mind, thanks be to God, but goin' on packin' up knowledge accordin' to her conscience: precept upon precept, line upon line; here a little, an' there a little. But (*with a passionate swing of her shawl*), thanks be to Christ, she knows when she was got, where she was got, an' how she was got; while there's some she knows, decoratin' their finger with a well-polished weddin' ring, would be hard put to it if they were assed to show their weddin' lines!

Mrs. Gogan (*plunging out into the centre of the floor in a wild tempest of hysterical rage*). Y' oul' rip of a blasted liar, me weddin' ring's been well earned be twenty years be th' side o' me husband, now takin' his rest in heaven, married to me be Father Dempsey, in th' Chapel o' Saint Jude's, in th' Christmas Week of eighteen hundhred an' ninety-five; an' any kid, livin' or dead, that Jinnie Gogan's had since, was got between th' bordhers of th' Ten Commandments! . . . An' that's more than some o' you can say that are kep' from th' dhread o' desthruction be a few drowsy virtues, that th' first whisper of temptation lulls into a sleep, that'll know one sin from another only on th' day of their last anointin', an' that use th' innocent light o' th' shinin' stars to dip into th' sins of a night's diversion!

Bessie (*jumping out to face* Mrs. Gogan, *and bringing the palms of her hands together in sharp claps to emphasize her remarks*). Liar to you, too, ma'am, y' oul' hardened thresspasser on other people's good nature, wizenin' up your soul in th' arts o' dodgeries, till every dhrop of respectability in a female is dhried up in her, lookin' at your ready-made manoeuverin' with th' menkind!

Rosie (*to* The Covey). It seems a highly rediculous thing to hear a thing that's only an inch or two away from a kid, swingin' heavy words about he doesn't know th' meanin' of, an' uppishly thryin' to down a man like Misther Fluther here, that's well flavoured in th' knowledge of th' world he's livin in.

The Covey (*savagely to* Rosie). Nobody's askin' you to be buttin' in with your prate. . . . I have you well taped, me lassie. . . . Just you keep your opinions for your own place. . . . It'll be a long time before Th' Covey takes any insthructions or reprimandin' from a prostitute!

Fluther (*to* Rosie). Houl' on there, Rosie; houl' on there. There's no necessity to flutther yourself when you're with Fluther. . . . Any lady that's in th' company of Fluther is goin' to get a fair hunt. . . . This is outside your province. . . . I'm not goin' to let you demean yourself be talkin' to a tittherin' chancer. . . . Leave this to Fluther—this is a man's job. (*To* The Covey) Now, if you've anything to say, say it to Fluther, an', let me tell you, you're not goin' to be pass-remarkable to any lady in my company.

The Covey. Sure I don't care if you were runnin' all night afther your Mary o' th' Curlin' Hair, but, when you start tellin' luscious lies about what you done for th' Labour movement, it's nearly time to show y'up!

Voice of Speaker. The last sixteen months have been the most glorious in the history of Europe. Heroism has come back to the earth. War is a terrible thing, but war is not an evil thing. People in Ireland dread war because they do not know it. Ireland has not known the exhilaration of war for over a hundred years. When war comes to Ireland she must welcome it as she would welcome the Angel of God!

Mrs. Gogan (*screaming*). Fluther, leggo! I'm not goin' to keep an unresistin' silence, an' her scattherin' her festherin' words in me face, stirrin' up every dhrop of decency in a respectable female, with her restless rally o' lies that would make a saint say his prayer backwards!

Bessie (*shouting*). Ah, everybody knows well that th' best charity that can be shown to you is to hide th' thruth as much as our thrue worship of God Almighty will allow us!

Mrs. Gogan (*frantically*). Here, houl' th' kid, one o' yous; houl' th' kid, you. (*Before* Peter *is aware of it, she places the infant in his arms*). . . . (*To* Bessie, *standing before her in a fighting attitude*). Come on, now, me loyal lassie, dyin' with grief for little Catholic Belgium! When Jinnie Gogan's done with you, you'll have a little leisure lyin' down to think an' pray for your king an' counthry!

Bessie (*as she goes out*). If you think, me lassie, that Bessie

Burgess has an untidy conscience, she'll soon show you to th' differ!

Fluther (*fiercely*). Is it you show Fluther up? G'way, man, I'd beat two o' you before me breakfast!

The Covey (*contemptuously*). Tell us where you bury your dead, will you?

Fluther (*with his face stuck into the face of* The Covey). Sing a little less on th' high note, or, when I'm done with you, you'll put a Christianable consthruction on things, I'm tellin' you!

The Covey. You're a big fella, you are.

Fluther (*tapping* The Covey *threateningly on the shoulder*). Now, you're temptin' Providence when you're temptin' Fluther!

The Covey (*losing his temper, and bawling*). Easy with them hands, there, easy with them hands! You're startin' to take a little risk when you commence to paw The Covey!
[Fluther *suddenly springs into the middle of the shop, flings his hat into the corner, whips off his coat, and begins to paw the air.*

Fluther (*roaring at the top of his voice*). Come on, come on, you lowser; put your mits up now, if there's a man's blood in you! Be God, in a few minutes you'll see some snots flyin' around, I'm tellin' you. . . . When Fluther's done with you, you'll have a vice versa opinion of him! Come on, now, come on!

The Covey (*struggling with the* Barman). Ay, leggo, leggo there; fair hunt, give a man a fair hunt! One minute with him is all I ask; one minute alone with him, while you're runnin' for th' priest an' th' doctor.

Fluther (*to the* Barman). Let him go, let him go, Tom! let him open th' door to sudden death if he wants to!

155

Voice of the Man. Our foes are strong, but strong as they are, they cannot undo the miracles of God, who ripens in the heart of young men the seeds sown by the young men of a former generation. They think they have pacified Ireland; think they have foreseen everything; think they have provided against everything; but the fools, the fools, the fools!—they have left us our Fenian dead, and, while Ireland holds these graves, Ireland, unfree, shall never be at peace!

WORKSHOP ACTIVITIES FOR ACT III

Act III is particularly striking from a purely theatrical point of view. There is hardly a pause for breath as people constantly enter and exit, guns explode, the soldiers retreat, the people loot shops, Nora becomes demented, Langon is mortally wounded, and Fluther drinks himself into a stupor and sings to the city's destruction.

At the centre of all this chaos one person finds he has to make an important decision. The enormous implications of his decision, the reasons for and against either alternative, are often overlooked. Clitheroe arrives on the scene with the wounded Langon and Brennan. Langon is pleading to be moved to an ambulance; Brennan is trying to persuade Clitheroe to forget about Nora, who is begging him to stay, and get a move on. Meanwhile Bessie shouts and jeers at them, as the guns go off in the background. It is a very emotive scene, charged with great energy and vitality. There is (as always when *reading* a play) a danger that students may interpret such a scene as being muddled and confused and so miss out on the importance of Clitheroe's predicament.

Here we see Clitheroe torn between personal and social imperatives. Should he desert the fight and, in turn, his comrades, for Nora? Is Nora asking too much? Is his final decision right or wrong? Can we say for certain, especially when we consider the immediate circumstances? The question was first presented in Act I: now Clitheroe is *forced* to decide.

It is worth trying to capture this conflict and the means by which O'Casey brings it to a climax. With the above considerations in mind, try to dramatise the section of Act III beginning with Brennan's 'Why did you fire over their heads? Why didn't you fire to kill? (line 526) and finishing on Fluther's 'Th' whole city can topple home to hell, for Fluther!' (line 697).

Speed is the essence of this scene. All the characters, apart from Bessie, are panic-stricken. Nora feels she will die if they leave; if they stay *they* will die; so they are arguing over life and death. Try to have each person start his or her line before the previous speaker has finished talking. And Clitheroe must at all times be kept as the central figure, being torn as he is by both sides. This can be done by having all the lines directed at Clitheroe, and having him move from one person to the other in his confusion.

As was pointed out before, the stage directions are the most reliable clues. For example, we are told that Brennan speaks *Fiercely to Clitheroe*; Nora *Imploringly*; and Langon *Agonizingly*. Though Clitheroe's words, as he pushes Nora away at the end, may seem to indicate that he is in a temper, this is unlikely. He has reached breaking point, and is really as weak as Nora. When he tells Brennan to 'Come on, come on', he does so in a state of desperation: another moment's delay and he might break down and cry.

Fluther's entrance should come after a moment's pause. His words act like a slow fading light after the hopeless chaos and confusion of the preceding events. An utter feeling of exhaustion prevails after so much energy has been exerted. We are left with what is to be the prevalent mood and atmosphere of Act IV.

WORKSHOP ACTIVITIES FOR ACT IV

Other than Bessie's death, there is really very little *action*, as such, in Act IV, its overall function being to bring into a single frame the net result of all that has happened in the preceding three acts. Nora has lost her child and is virtually insane; Clitheroe has been killed; Mollser has finally succumbed to consumption; while the remaining characters are little changed or affected. In many ways, then, Act IV is a summing up.

But a play rarely comes to a single conclusion: in the end we are left with the characters in the play and what we think they might feel at this point. So what do they feel? What are their ideas?

In this respect there is an interesting exercise that students who have studied the whole play may like to try their hands at. And this is to attempt a summing up of the events in the play as seen through the eyes of any one character in the play. In other words, to write out the story of the play, including the most relevant incidents, as told by, for example, Nora or Fluther—and, most importantly, having these characters express their personal opinions. Because no two characters share precisely the same attitudes or regard things in the same light, each description should be unique.

Describing the meeting in Act II, Peter for instance would be likely to concentrate on the great excitement that was generated, while The Covey would say what a boring meeting it was. On the other hand

Nora, who did not see the meeting, might talk about how she sat with Mollser all through the night, listening to the sounds of the crowds outside, and thinking all the time of her husband and what might happen to him if there *was* an armed insurrection, etc.

The important thing is to make sure that the character from whose point of view you are writing is consistent with that of the same character in the play. Any number of students may work together on one character, or different students may depict the same character but be concerned with only one act.

Should this prove rewarding, there is a second and more interesting stage. Separate groups of students, using material from the previous exercise, could compile a kind of dossier on one character, consisting of the most typical kinds of things that character would say. By familiarising themselves with this dossier they gain a rough idea of how such and such a character thinks: in other words, they are learning to identify with him or her. It is now possible to set up an *improvisation*, with one person from each group playing the part of one or other of the characters in the play.

The improvisation can take the form of a discussion. There is no limit to the number of topics they may discuss, and there are no rules as to the direction the discussion should take. (A list of suggested topics is given at the end of this section.) Nor is it necessary to place all the characters together. Any combination is of equal interest. Students may then want to improvise actual sections from the play itself, that is, taking a single incident from the play—Nora and Jack arguing at the end of Act I, for example—and allowing it to develop in any direction.

The secret of improvisation is that, given a small amount of information about a character in the play, a student, given total freedom, may then go on to discover aspects of that character that may never have occurred to him or her from merely reading the play. But it is important too to encourage as much discussion as possible after such sessions, to have students who are watching take notes, and to have accounts of some description from all students, detailing what they feel they have or have not learned.

Possible topics for improvised discussion
1. *Ireland unfree shall never be at peace.*
2. *A woman should be happy to see her husband going to fight for his country.*
3. *God bless the Citizen Army.*
4. *Workers' rights before nationalism.*
5. *There's no such thing as an Irishman.*

6. *A lot o' vipers, that's what the Irish is.*
7. *Slavery is better than bloodshed.*
8. *It's all the fault of the English.*
9. *Wearing a fancy green costume is the best way to demonstrate your loyalty to Ireland.*
10. *Is there anybody goin' with a titther o' sense?*